You'll Land on Your Feet

How *Anyone* Can Survive and Thrive After Job Loss

André W. Renna, BSIE, MBA

authorHOUSE®

AuthorHouse™
1663 Liberty Drive
Bloomington, IN 47403
www.authorhouse.com
Phone: 1-800-839-8640

First published by AuthorHouse 3/8/2011

ISBN: 978-1-4567-3084-0 (e)
ISBN: 978-1-4567-3085-7 (dj)
ISBN: 978-1-4567-3086-4 (sc)

Library of Congress Control Number: 2011901660

Printed in the United States of America

*To my wife Patricia for her unwavering support,
patience, and tireless review of the text.*

*To my children, Christopher and Christine, and son-
in-law, Aaron, for their confidence in my abilities
and encouragement to complete the book.*

*In memory of my mother and father, Alma and William Renna, who
instilled the moral fortitude to persevere through life's challenges and
to appreciate the importance of family. They are sorely missed.*

Table of Contents

Introduction

"Write the book! Write the book! Write the book! It needs to be written, WRITE THE DARN BOOK!" That is my lovely wife "encouraging me" through the "opportunity" given to me by my employer of over 20 years as they "thanked" me for my tremendous contributions, my positive impact on the organization and the legacy I will leave as they informed me that my position had been eliminated. Oh yeah, by the way, *"the empty boxes in your 'old' office are for your legacy"* (that was the HR person, not my wife).

So, after a few months of sorting through the "what just happened" phase, the "outplacement assistance" phase (or as I refer to it, as a Catholic, the alternative to the company saying five Our Fathers and ten Hail Marys), and the intense networking or "how about lunch" phase, I am writing this book. It is probably worthwhile to establish the approach of the book and clarify expectations (yours and mine—mostly yours):

- First, I like bullet points (case in point—bullet points already)
- Second, I am a 56 year old "out placed" senior executive who anticipated retiring from the company I loved and was passionate about for 21 years
- Third, I grew up in Brooklyn, have Italian American heritage, (I can sense the stereotyping already) therefore have an inherent language impediment (so my wife says) so if you are looking for a Harvard Business Review articulation, stop now. I promise to use #*#*# when I am really emphasizing a point (in case your kids pick up the book). I am also apt to emphasize a point using the exclamation, *"OOOOHHHH!"* (To be said like Paulie Walnuts from the Soprano's)
- Fourth, I have an engineering degree, an MBA, and have been in

manufacturing, retail, healthcare, and consumer food products, large and small business. I even worked as a shipping clerk in the Bowery in NY when I first graduated with a B.S. from Syracuse University during the Carter years. I am not a writer (which you may have figured out already) but I believe I have some perspective which you may find interesting, and even helpful.

- Fifth, although I do not profess to be an expert in what I am presenting, I have one credential which qualifies me to present this content—these are my reflections of what I have gone through since being dumped (OOOOHHHH! that was how my mother referred to my situation to her 80 year old friends from the old neighborhood…gotta love her!). I do not have to get approval by a committee, Board member, or CEO, to share this information in the format I chose (wow! That was liberating). Of course my wife has approved everything I wrote.

- Sixth, even at the time of writing this book, I am still not completely "over" having lost my position (which I believe you will find is not unusual). If you detect occasional sarcasm and/or bitterness in some of the dialogue, then obviously you are sharp as a tack, however, it is my intent to minimize these elements.

- Seventh, this book is not simply a "how to" book on starting over, finding a new career, "be all that you can be", blah blah blah. It is also being written in the hope that it might shed some light on what we (the outplaced) go through. And, that you are not alone…not by any stretch.

- Eighth, I am not a psychiatrist, preacher, or Zig Ziglar. This book is not designed to heal your pain, have you spring off the couch to face new challenges, or find a higher purpose. All good things if they occur, but not a guarantee that comes with the book.

- Ninth, If I accomplish my objective (still in exec mode) you will be nodding your head (north/south, or east/west), smiling, saying, "uh huh, yep" or even laughing. If I was still on an incentive plan, your laughter would be "Exceeds Expectations", valued at 125% of the objective (those of you who were on classic performance incentive programs can relate).

- Tenth, I was going to stop at nine, but I notice there is a tenth point…I like to use parenthesis and quotation marks.

Make no mistake about it, I am not making light of a situation that is life altering and impacts your entire family. What I am doing is giving you something to pick up now and then and hopefully bring a smile to your face and the recognition that you are not alone. For many, that will not suffice to get them through the day, for some, it may.

This book will also address the phases of transition that you may be experiencing and shed some light on what you can expect. It is not research based other than my "findings" from those I have encountered along my journey (oh yeah, that's a big word in this process—*"Journey"*. It's the positive way to refer to the trip which you never planned to take).

As you take this journey you will be encouraged by many who will say, *"I Know You'll Land on Your Feet"*. Your visceral reaction to this polite comment must be tempered as their intent to "boost you up" is probably genuine, but lacks the understanding of the state of the "real" world in which you will be taking your *"journey"*. Perhaps we will "Land on our Feet", when we recognize that the normalcy in our life has changed and we just need to understand, accept and even embrace it.

I hope that reading "You'll Land on Your Feet" brings some cathartic reflection, a brighter moment in your day, and ultimately, softens your landing. I wish you well.

It's Not You, It's Us

*"If you have <u>integrity</u>, nothing else matters. If you don't
have integrity, nothing else matters"* ~Alan Simpson

There are a number of ways people find out about their "destiny"— the elimination of their position. Some may have expected it, but most, I imagine, did not, particularly if you have had acceptable or even stellar performance reviews, have not stolen from the company, whacked a supervisor, or slept with the boss's spouse. You were probably just doing your job when you received that "odd" message to come to the "bosses" office or the head of HR (if your boss needed someone else to do the dirty work).

Some would have expected a routine update, while others were anxious about the spontaneous and urgent need to meet. In my case, my administrative assistant had received a request by the COO, whom I reported to, that I was to clear my schedule and be available the next day (Wednesday) at 9:15 A.M. The COO was leaving for vacation and wanted to meet with me before she left on Wednesday evening. Not an unusual request for a COO to meet with a Senior V.P. before they left town, except, this COO *never* felt that urgency before. So, even my administrative assistant thought it was odd. But, be that as it may, I cleared my schedule and assumed it was going to be just a benign encounter.

However, working late on Tuesday, the evening before the "scheduled meeting", I noticed that the COO's office light was on. Having planned to make a presentation to one of my many departments at 7:00 A.M. on Wednesday, I thought I would inform the COO so we were aligned on the operational communication that the staff would be receiving.

I stopped by the office and discussed the presentation; there was no issue as we had previously evaluated the action. I took the opportunity to ask about the topic for discussion when we meet on Wednesday so that I could be prepared to discuss. After evading the subject, (*"we'll just talk tomorrow"*), the COO finally stated that there had been some ongoing organizational structure evaluation underway which she would like to share with me. As a senior member of the leadership team, I was not involved in those "organizational evaluation discussions". OOOOHHHH! Probably missed a clue there!

This would not have been so suspect had the blood not rushed from the COO's face and a grim reaper expression develop. As I acknowledged our time to meet in the morning, and said goodnight, it struck me..."Wait, something's not right here". I turned back and asked, appearing somewhat cavalier (which was more a defense mechanism than a comfort level) "do I have a job"? Imagine her surprise at the candid question. Imagine my surprise at the answer..."you better sit down". (Ok, here is a defining moment in life).

After a 30 second explanation by someone I have worked with over the past 15 years as a peer, friend, then as a subordinate, I suddenly became "employee number 12345". "Well, we have decided to restructure, your position is eliminated, I will get the Sr.V.P. of HR, she will explain" (I guess that is actually less than 30 seconds unless you come from the South and speak really slowly!).

Then the uncomfortable and dramatic pause, until the entrance of the CDO, Chief Development Officer (who had been with the company less than one year). The CDO's compassionate opening line was *"only you can throw us off our schedule, we were planning to speak with you tomorrow"*. My immediate thought was "that's your opening line with respect to this life altering event …you've got to be kidding me"?!! Did she expect me to say, "Oh, I am so sorry to trouble you. How insensitive of me. Do you want me to come back tomorrow so you can fire me on schedule"? I held my tongue and said nothing since everything I wanted to say would have come out in "Brooklyn-ese", accompanied by Italian hand gestures.

That stellar opening line was followed by the classic diversionary tactic, "*It's not you, It's us.*" Not sure what that means, but there was more to come: "*You have done an outstanding job and have been a valued employee for years*"; "*This is not personal*". That one kills me, well then can you tell me what the heck is more personal than being dumped? (Thanks mom for the expression!). And then the coup de' gras (are you sitting down?)...."*your legacy is substantial at the organization*", "*what you have accomplished for the community and the organization will have impact into the future*".

Wow! I wonder how many of you, at that point, were satisfied with the fact that your legacy would live on, and your contributions, would succeed you? If that scripted line wasn't as disingenuous and stated as if read from a teleprompter, it might have softened the devastating realization, that at 55, I would be looking for a new job. Does any of this sound familiar?

Before exiting the COO office to discuss the "generous" (depends on who's perspective) severance package, the final cliché (which I am grateful for at this time) was offered. (Drum roll, please)... "*I Know You Will Land on Your Feet*".

Look, let's get something straight early on in the "journey" through this book: *it is management's prerogative to change structure and to eliminate positions.* There is need for a process and a consistent approach to confronting those of us who will be "severed" so as to protect the organization from any appearance of discrimination or constructive discharge. I get it. We all need to accept that. But, there are right ways and wrong ways to discharge employees, particularly those that have been contributing for decades and have had extraordinary level of commitment and loyalty to the organization (the "legacy club"). From the "research" (again recall the research is my personal interactions); it appears that many companies have just not come close to handling the discharges in a compassionate and professional manner.

I was actually fortunate. Others that were "eliminated" at my organization on the following day (remember I screwed up THEIR plans),

3

were exposed to a harsher situation. They were escorted back to their office where empty boxes had been pre-constructed for them to pack their belongings. Oh yeah…their peers, subordinates and friends, were at their work stations uncomfortably observing the "farewell". Some legacy and way to be remembered! I hope your fate was better. It is never going to be easy to be displaced, but there should be some recognition of the employee's dignity during the encounter. The bitterness that is felt at the time , and will resurface again and again, is not only due to the outcome…no job, but I believe (as many have told me), the lasting effect of how it was handled that infamous day.

So, if you think your situation was unique and that you got blind-sided and humiliated, keep in mind that it appears to be the way most of our last days went. At some point, you will need to deal with it and understand it *really wasn't you*; just some leadership team that believes they are doing the right thing for the many by sacrificing the few. And, unfortunately due to a lack of corporate compassion, a shortage of messengers that are skilled in empathy, coupled with a general concern of potential legal action by the employee, the likelihood of a well delivered "discharge" is slim.

Table 1: U.S. Unemployment Statistics, Sept. 2010

- Unemployment in the U.S. is 9.6%
- Number of unemployed is 14.8 million
- Number of long-term unemployed (over 27 weeks) is 6.1 million
- 1486 employers had mass layoffs involving 133,379 workers
- Regional unemployment:
  1. West, 10.99%
  2. Midwest, 9.3%
  3. South, 9.2%
  4. Northeast, 8.6%
- States with highest unemployment (top 5):
  1. Nevada, 14.4%
  2. Michigan, 13.0 %

3. California, 12.4%
4. Florida, 11.9%
5. Rhode Island, 11.5%
- Unemployment for select industries:
    1. Construction, 17.2%
    2. Leisure and Hospitality, 11.4%
    3. Professional and Business Services, 9.9%
    4. Manufacturing, 9.6%
    5. Transportation, 7.7%
    6. Education Services, 7.5%
    7. Healthcare Services, 6.0%
    8. Utilities, 3.8%

"The beauty of the soul shines out when a man bears with composure one heavy mischance after another, not because he does not feel them, but because he is a man of high and heroic temper" ~**Aristotle**

Bitter? I'm Not Bitter...I'm Pissed!

*"Forego your anger for a moment and save yourself
a hundred ways of trouble"* ~Chinese Proverb

That day, or night when you return home, you have the very difficult task of telling your family, particularly your spouse (a term which may be politically incorrect, but hopefully does not cause you to toss the book at this point), that you "plan to sleep in tomorrow morning!" Some chose to call their spouse immediately upon exiting the company parking lot (as in my case). Others wait to get home first and address face-to-face upon their arrival.

Some hope to avoid communicating the news until the "right time' (whenever the heck that might be). One individual who I know, drove home (he was released in the morning), and as he was driving, he actually passed his wife driving in the opposite direction. When she immediately cell phoned him after they passed, he bailed out and said he had a meeting on the other side of town toward their home. He could not even inform her that evening, but eventually had to "man up" the next morning. I would not be surprised if some hold-off days before telling their spouse. Not sure where they go each day until they 'fess up", but that is none of my business.

No matter when you do it, it will rip at your gut. So, I figure, the sooner the better. It is probably one of the hardest things you will have to do. This is a normal reaction to an unpleasant situation. I don't know what the psychologists would say, but no matter how small, or large your ego is, facing the reality of being "discharged' is not easy. Hopefully, you have family, and friends who are supportive, compassionate and empathetic. Some may even be in the same situation–perhaps you can "*journey*" together!

Your first reaction, the defense mechanism we all have, will be to recoil and not want to broadcast your situation. Whether that is driven by your ego, your natural tendency to avoid uncomfortable discourse, or your still being in a state of disbelief, you must get passed that. Every outplacement advisor and recruitment professional (to be discussed in Chapter 6) that is ready to guide those of us on our "journey", will counsel you on the importance of letting people know that you are unemployed, available, and (by all previous indications of the leaders that let you go), a tremendous asset to any organization.

You will receive sage advice (which will be so counter intuitive to your urge to lash out), "*You must shed your bitterness and put a positive spin on the course of events.*" OOOOHHHH! Do they know I just got screwed? Are they freakin' kidding me? They will advise you to practice saying such things as, "I had a fine run at the company and am grateful for that", "this is an opportunity for me to do something which I have always wanted to do", "this is not an end, but a new beginning", "as this door closes a new window opens" (any of these sound familiar?). Well, that sounds outstanding, except what we are thinking is more like, "I am really not bitter... I am pissed" That's right I said it..."I AM PISSED". And I may be pissed for a really long time. I may never end being pissed. That's my prerogative. So put all the lipstick on this pig that you want–it is what it is. New beginning, closed doors, opened windows...who am I? 14 years old and just got dumped by my girlfriend?!

I too recommend that before you go back out in the real world, certainly before you interact with potential business associates and future referral sources, that you get it under control. I don't mean just controlling the anger, and there WILL be anger, but your dialogue, even dialogue that *appears* to be said when you are composed.

As I mentioned, I am a New Yorker, a third generation Italian-American. Emotion and animation are part of my genetic composition. Dialogue, supplemented by hand movement and an occasional

"Fuggedaboutit" were a part of my every day communication (outside of the professional setting....well, for the most part). So, for me to be devoid of emotion and let this all "pass" was probably as difficult as it would be for anyone. But, with the help of my wife, children and friends (and of course mom), I did OK with the emotion. BUT, I really struggled with the "what to say" aspect for a long time. It wasn't a "high road, low road" issue for me, but more of a concern that it minimized the life changing circumstance that my family was now faced with. It made it appear that the "journey" was to be embraced and no big deal, even though the United States was experiencing one of the worst economic times in our history (in addition to my being 55 years old). *I had a great deal of trouble getting past that.*

My demeanor of *"how* to say it" (calm, non-threatening–without biting my hand–that's an Italian thing) started improving around the second month or so. But my wording, my phraseology, still left a lot to be desired. I am not proud of how long it took me to "adjust", and I would urge you to "fast forward" that part of the journey. You absolutely need to get that under control early as it does not speak well of you as a leader, and in some situations could even eliminate opportunities. From a practical side, it can potentially jeopardize your severance (that AMAZING package that the company gave you out of the kindness of their heart, the one without the gold watch for retiring gracefully).

Let me clarify. Instead of saying, *"Yes, I hoped to retire from this company, but I guess someone else had other plans for me"* (my early response), a more advantageous response would have been, *"Yes, it is unfortunate, but I had a very good career and learned a great deal which I can apply elsewhere"*, or, *"My talents and experiences have prepared me for many options, so I am taking some time to evaluate and develop a plan for my future"*. I must admit (now) those later words sound much better and reflect the characteristics that are needed in a leader.

As I said, the professionals will tell you to let it go, shed your bitterness and move on. I say, you earned the right to be bitter. I don't know anyone that has been in this situation without experiencing anger, disdain and being down right pissed off. Just don't let it get the best of you and manifest into a damaging attitude and presence. If you do that then, as a physician friend of mine counseled me, "you let the big uglies win" (he said it in Latin and it sounded better, but this was basically the message).

You can create a significant level of personal damage to your image and "hire-ability" by how you communicate after the discharge, especially for those in leadership positions. It is *essential*, as hard as it may be, to refrain from self-destructing. Remember, it may not have been "you" that created the predicament you are now in, but it is ALL you with regard to how you are perceived after the discharge.

I thought I knew what my physician friend was saying when he first called me and said, "*Don't get sick over this*", (mom said that repeatedly also), but it took me awhile to really figure it out. What he was saying was don't let them change who you are. Don't let them cause you to be a self doubter and, maybe worse, a vindictive, negative person. You may think you have lost your dignity, but you haven't. Not by the "discharge" action. But, if you are not careful, your bitterness will transcend to being chronically pissed off (I think that's a medical term, CPO), and will only hurt you and complicate what you are trying to do—change your life and "land softly". I wish I had taken my own advice earlier as I look back and think of all the first encounters which I could have done differently, better. Be pissed, you earned that right, but be smart, no one really wants to talk to or hire a pissed off individual.

> *"Self control is the quality that distinguishes the fittest to survive"* ~**George Bernard Shaw**

Here's His Belongings

"While grief is fresh, every attempt to divert only irritates.
You must wait till it be digested, and then amusement
will dissipate the remains of it" ~Samuel Johnson

As I had mentioned earlier, one of the hardest aspects of this change is to tell your loved ones that your life is about to take an unexpected turn. I have spoken to so many individuals who have expressed that their family, particularly their spouse, was as devastated as they, if not more; although they are supportive, they too are going through a range (or is it rage) of emotions, including the heartbreak of seeing you distraught and struggling. Don't ever forget this. You are not the only one affected by this change. There is a sense of loss for those who care most about you. Understand that they need support as well and it is eating them up inside to see their husband, wife, mother, father, son or daughter in pain.

My outplacement advisor noted early on that I would be going through a process similar to the "stages of grief". Having recently lost a number of friends and relatives, including my father and, during the process of writing this book, my mother, I certainly understand the stages of grief. But I thought this was some stretch if she was trying to create a metaphor around death. Give me break. Cut the drama. But for most, this may be the case, even if you don't realize it at the time.

You may have expected this to be your "job for life". So when things change you will experience many different emotions. Since we are all different, you may not experience exactly what your friend did but the range of emotions will be similar. They are normal.. Be wary as you go from phase to phase and don't be averse to seeking professional help and guidance if you linger in the "Worry" and "Depression" phases.

Table 2: Stages of Grief

- **Shock**—What did they just say?!
- **Denial**—This really can't be happening, not to me!
- **Anger**—Those bastards will get theirs (Karma).
- **Worry**—Now what do I do, what about my family?
- **Depression**—There is no way out of this mess, why bother.
- **Resistance**—I'm not changing.
- **Acceptance**—OK, this sucks but time to move on and not give up.
- **Action**—Got a plan. I'm on it. This too shall pass.

And then something happened. My wife owned a business and one day, my former executive assistant (we'll call her "Sally") came into the business; and presented my wife with a box of items from my office which I had not taken. "Sally" said, and I quote, *"Here are André's belongings"*! When do you usually hear the term "belongings"? Yeah, that's right, when the person is deceased!

My wife said it was like the air was sucked from her lungs and she was speechless (I'm going to let that one go since she proofs my writing!). Knowing my assistant for years, my wife knew this was not someone trying to be cute or certainly not mean spirited. It was just a term she used to acknowledge that "I was no longer with the team", I was gone. And her reference was telling.

I felt horrible for my wife as she said for a moment she had an awful eerie feeling come over her. She said it was though I had died; I suspect a part of me did. And then we both started to reflect: many people sent us cards noting their disbelief, their sadness and regrets that I was "gone". They continued by saying that their thoughts and prayers were with us. I even received a couple of bouquets of flowers at my home. And, many phone calls from ex-staff, business associates and even board members.

Often times my wife would get the call if I was out networking. Holy crap, maybe I am dead!

The outpouring by so many was heart - warming and unexpected. My wife and I shared, "this is like watching your own funeral'. Melodramatic, perhaps, but none the less, it felt like a dry run for my passing, without the black suit and make up!

I was relaying this to a friend of mine who had a very interesting perspective which stuck with me. When one passes away you really don't know the impact you may have had on others. You wonder sometimes, geez, if I die, would anyone come to the funeral? Especially if it's pouring rain (this is the true test!). He said I was fortunate to be able to see how people reached out to my family - and me (since technically I was still alive). Most people never experience that. As odd as it sounds, his comment resonated with me enough that I decided to include it in the book (plus he bought lunch and I owe him).

We get so tied up with our busy lives that we don't stop to ponder how we impact those around us. We go through our days doing what we were hired to do, determined to succeed, and working as it was instilled in us by our parents, never really grasping how we may have touched someone. This may be especially true if you are a compassionate and influential person or leader. To be clear, I am not writing this to say... "wow, look at me, I will be missed more than the Chicago Bulls missed Michael Jordan". That's not it. My point is simply this; reflect on the good that you left behind; the lives that you touched, the impact that you had. People care and some do understand what you are going through.

When you are feeling down and thinking, "What did I do wrong?" Or, "How did I screw up?" Pull out one of those "Thinking of You" letters, or, recall conversations or times when you may have positively influenced or helped mentor someone. Remember, you are still very much alive. And, in time, you will re-energize and move forward, unless you allow yourself to linger in that self-deprecating victim world. Don't let this be your "funeral", and for heaven sake, don't let the "uglies" beat you.

Another friend of mine, who was going through the same "journey", was struggling very much and stated "*This is like dying a thousand* deaths". He would say, *"This is not the way it's supposed to be. I worked hard for 35 years and now at 55 (odd coincidence in age?), there isn't a damn thing out there for me. I am not sleeping and some mornings I have no idea why I am getting up".* I know he is not unique in this feeling. I agreed, *"yeah no doubt this sucks beyond comprehension and unfortunately bad things happen to good people, but you can't give up and watch your life go by".* If this is how you are feeling, consider volunteering at a human service agency or program in your neighborhood. There is nothing more rewarding then contributing your time and experience as you continue your search for your next employment opportunity.

There are so many of us in this situation and to think that everyone will land where they once were is just wishful thinking (originally I was going to say delusional, but *"wishful"* sounds better). So, adjustments in your life may be the order of the day. Put the ego aside, or what's left of it, and "gather your belongings" and work on a plan. Stay close to the people who have reached out to you, recognize that this impacts more than just you, and reflect upon all the good that you have encountered along the way. And for the love of Pete (hopefully not the name of the guy who "dumped" you) don't forget how to laugh. Try to find humor where you can. As hard as this sounds, it will help get you through the journey.

While bringing my "belongings" to my wife was pretty intense at the time, now when she thinks of it she smiles and asks, "is that all you left me? Cheap bastard!"

> **"I love the man that can smile in trouble, that can gather strength from distress, and grow brave by reflection." ~Thomas Paine**

You're "Lucky" You Don't Work Here Anymore!

"Our most difficult task as a friend is to offer understanding when we don't understand" ~Robert Brault

Chapter 3 talked about the grieving process, and your "passing". But it also talked about the positive aspect of some people reaching out, maybe those you never expected , to say "good luck", "hang in there", and the dreaded (but heartfelt) "I know you will land on your feet". If you had these experiences then you know what I am talking about. It got you through some days and restored your faith in people, well SOME people.

The flip-side, and I am willing to bet that many of you experienced this, is the obvious omission of "compassion and outreach" from some, particularly, if you were a leader, by the peers you worked closely with for years. These may be your "work friends", and perhaps you did not do a great deal socially together, but, you spent hours solving problems, exchanging life stories and supporting each other through tough times as they related to business. You may have even helped each other through tough personal times.

You knew their spouse, watched their children grow up, heard all the parenting horror stories, and the sick parents stories. And now you are separated from the "old crew". That in itself sucks. But you know that you had some great time together and are sure they will keep in touch.

Delusion number two. One of the greatest disappointments in this entire journey has been the disappearance of those who remained. For some of us, it is mind boggling that "friends" can vanish.

In most cases (I don't have data to say *all* cases) it becomes "policy" to not contact the "displaced". Circumstances exist that create fear for those who "made the cut". Contacting one of the "severed" may not be appreciated by those who made the decision. At first, I thought, "They must be so uncomfortable not knowing what to say, that they just cannot touch base". I started to feel bad for them (well, maybe just a little). Then as time passes, you realize something just isn't right. Then the possibility sinks in that these people either never cared much about you (which I like to believe is unlikely), or they were subtly, or maybe directly, told that it would not be in their best interest to remain in contact with the displaced. I have spoken to others who have absolutely confirmed that, not only did they experience the same "Houdini" acts by those they considered peers and friends, but it was confirmed that keeping in touch was "ixnay".

Now, I understand that those left behind would not want to jeopardize their careers by having a continuous ongoing conversation with the "dead". But how do you not contact someone, even if by sending a quick note, or a brief call, to say "I enjoyed working together, I wish you luck, and (heaven forbid), feel free to contact me once you decide what your game plan is". That doesn't take much time, does it? To avoid any chance for the ex-employee to vent or try and engage the caller in a long conversation, just send a freakin' note!

I am of the school that there is a right way and a wrong way to treat friends and associates. I bet your mom told you that as a child. And for those that are too uncomfortable to deal with the situation, what the heck are they doing in a leadership position?! Perhaps it is as Aristotle stated, *"Man by nature is a political animal"*.

Again, could be you (or I) had an overestimation of your relationships. Only you would know. But when so many reach out and *none* are from your peer group, that speaks volumes about the corporate culture you left behind, a recognition of a culture of fear. When organizations preach "ethics and a culture of respect for the individual" (which is written in practically every mission credo since 2000) this certainly appears to be counter cultural or perhaps it's a reflection of "ethical erosion".

One might say, "If you feel that passionate, why don't *you* call *them*"? That crosses one's mind, but can you imagine how awkward it would be for those you called, when they have been told, or perceive, that contact with you can be harmful to their health? (HMMMM…that's a *"ponderable"*, maybe we *should* pick up the phone…..). I am not going to dwell on this issue. I just have heard of so many instances where people were asked "did you hear from "so and so". When they are told that they haven't, the person asking is startled; "I thought you guys were buds, or didn't you help him get his job, or didn't you work closely on projects"? This is usually followed by "unbelievable!" Hear that a few times and you start to think, maybe I was not delusional to think a friendly peer would reach out.

I'm thinking that some individuals are going to put self preservation before what should be the right thing to do. As I have said before, you need to accept this truth and move on. If you happen to run into them again, are you going to give them a big hug and slap on the back and chat about the good old days like nothing happened? Or are you going to walk right past them and say "you're dead to me!" (not sure which Italian mob movie that came from but you know it has to be in a few). Do you "play the game" or do you sink to their level? You decide where the happy medium is, but keep the discussion in Chapter 2 in mind and perhaps the following quote from Alan Simpson (you may have read this at the beginning of Chapter One), *"If you have integrity, nothing else matters, if you don't have integrity, nothing else matters".*

My closing thought is, "What goes around, comes around" (something my wife learned from her parents). We now refer to this as "Karma". This thought can certainly help get you through the day!

I think it is very hard to have lost your job after so many years of commitment and loyalty. Would you agree? It is as though you are an outcast, voted off the island and some of your business "friends", especially those who are fearful of losing their jobs through association, have shunned you. And if that's not bad enough, in the midst of feeling like you have hit the bottom, some genius, in an attempt to "cheer you up", suggests, *"You have no idea how lucky you are to be out of here. You should count your blessings that you don't have to be at this place every day."* So I'm thinking, I see–of course–how foolish of me–I am FORTUNATE, and need to look at this with the right perspective: I lost the position I loved in an organization I had hoped to retire from, I am 55 and *everyone* is looking for a 55 year old to hire, the economy is stable, there are plenty of jobs out there (at the time of this chapter U.S. unemployment broke 10%), lost my life insurance and long-term disability the company provided, can no longer contribute to a 401 K(or 403b plan) , will not accrue additional pension, lost my ability to refinance my home (no job!), have health insurance for a short period, and then blessed with the opportunity to purchase COBRA at multiples of what I paid as an employee for health insurance, I now need to revise my retirement planning, have to face my family and friends and explain why I have the opportunity each morning to watch Regis and Kelly, and have a pit in my stomach that hopefully won't develop into an ulcer, and for many, a cash flow problem (hopefully you prepared for a rainy day–or year). What the heck was I thinking?!...I am *so lucky* to have been given the opportunity to take this journey. I may even write a freakin' thank you note to the people who decided that I was better off. Maybe I'll get my wife and kids to sign it and ask my nieces and nephews to draw pictures representing each of the elements of joy that this event has produced. We can make a damn calendar out of it!

I am sure people believe they are helping or commiserating with you by telling you "you are better off". My answer to them is— how about if I decide what is best for me and my family. You have no idea unless you have been in my shoes what effect this has on us. Or as my wife suggested I say in response, *"Really? Want to switch places?!"*

You may agree, in your particular case that the organization is not what is used to be, should be or could be. But, under these circumstances how anyone can say "you are better off" is just beyond me. I don't believe they are mean spirited and they may even truly believe your being separated is heaven sent, but this is NOT what you care to hear after a life altering event.

So, if you have friends that mean well, print this chapter for them and send it with a nice card saying, "Let me know when you decide to leave this place and be *better off* so I can send you a congratulations card!"

> *"Nothing but heaven itself is better than a*
> *friend who is really a friend".* ~Plautus

Now What Do I Do?

"Never give in, never give in, never, never, never, never - in nothing, great or small, large or petty - never give in except to convictions of honor and good sense." ~Winston Churchill

Sooner or later the initial shock starts to wear off and reality starts to set in. You have gone through the "this is surreal" phase and "I'll wake up from this bad dream" delusion to recognize that as Frank Barone would say in Everybody Loves Raymond, "Holy Crap", "I have no job and I'm old" (well, old in relation to how young you used to be and how old you are feeling lately!) You wake up one morning and look in the mirror and it hits you, "Now what do I do?"

You think, "For 20 years I got up, had my morning coffee, said goodbye to the spouse and kids, traveled to work, listened to the same radio station on the way, said 'good morning' to the same people as I entered the same building, and picked up where I left off the day before." Seems mundane, but it was what you did, what you (may have) planned to do until you retired. It was a part of your life that was grounded, or at least you thought so. Now what will a day look like? When does it begin, when does the day end? What gets accomplished in between? Who will I interact with throughout the day? Will I need to relocate? Will I need to change professions? Will I drive my spouse crazy (later chapter!). This is a real "Holy Crap"! You conclude: "I know, I'll seek advice from my friends. They have always been a great support and "sounding board". Then reality hits, "Oh wait, dummy, they're ALL AT WORK! And some of them have me on the "persona non grata self-preservation list". This sucks!

But, I am strong, I am invincible, I am man (or woman). And yet, I don't know where the heck to start. Maybe Oprah can help! Oh No! I just turned the TV channel to Oprah! Quick! Somebody smack me!

If you've entered into the, "Now What Do I Do?" days. You know exactly what I mean. If you haven't–you will. Assuming most of you reading this were energetic, high achievers and still very productive in your organization, you are going to develop a glazed over look, the proverbial deer in the headlights. You will know what I mean when your "better half" starts snapping their fingers to see if anybody is home (they may not notice the difference if you never responded to him/her in the past but I will assume you were responsive prior to the start of your "*journey*").

Even those that coasted the last couple of years are going to be thrown off by the amount of "what to do now" time. You had a routine, some consistency throughout the day and work week. It is important to develop a "new routine" early in the process, and get that purpose and process for accomplishment back on track. Some key elements of establishing a new routine include:

- Develop objectives and stay focused. Give yourself targets for certain milestones.
- Establish reasonable expectations to avoid disappointment. Do research, including talking with other executives, those who have had the same experience, as well as your outplacement professional. Understand the normal time it takes to make such a life change, or to "land".
- Create your own new structure. Create a To- Do list (to be discussed later). Become disciplined in order to prevent becoming aimless, complacent and proliferating a "victim" mentality. Develop short and long term goals and treat them like any project goals you established…they are just as important!!!
- Talk to your spouse, family and friends. Particularly your spouse. You need to be open and honest and share your thoughts and

listen. Establish some early expectations of what this process will bring. The amount of time, what you are willing to accept, how you will interact through the process. This journey will (probably) be long and bumpy.

- Come to grips with what happened and develop a clear statement to share with others when asked. This (as mentioned above) is critical to your being able to move on and show your leadership character.
- Don't become discouraged with your new routine. Finding a new career will take time and patience. It is a full time job if you are committed. Balance your urge to "just land" with the objective of finding that real opportunity which you can truly embrace, become passionate about.

Some of us were *fortunate* (to be said with a distinctive degree of sarcasm) to have "outplacement services" made available (this oddly named service will be discussed in the next chapter). This gives us a "place to go" (which doesn't include the horses, slot machines or Texas Hold'em tables) and some "programmatic Stepford approach" to planning the journey. But, what if you don't have one of these oases to visit during your journey? Well, I guess it's up to you to pull it together, sit yourself down and take out a blank sheet of paper and develop your trip plan (it would be great if you could just call AAA for a Trip Tik but it's a bit more complicated than that).

There are many tips and resources that you should consider to help you through the days ahead. Listed in Table 3 are just a few of the many tools that are available, most for zero cost. Again, some are given access to services which offer assistance in many of these areas. But as I will review in the next chapter, make no mistake about it, it is up to you! No one can do this for you. So if you haven't gotten started, now would be a great time. It wouldn't offend me if you put down the book for a few days!

Noted below is a partial checklist of the many resources available to you to assist in the planning, marketing and researching for your next position. With time and patience, you can expand this list by surfing the web and soliciting input from friends and colleagues.

Table 3: Resource Checklist

- Small Business Administration (SBA)
- Small Business Development Centers (SBDC) at your local colleges and universities
- Local and state Chamber of Commerce and Industry
- Service Corps of Retired Executives (SCORE)
- Directories and Publications such as:
    1. American Financial Directory
    2. Directory of Corporate Affiliation
    3. Directory of American Firms Operating in Foreign Countries
    4. Directory of Foreign Firms Operating in the U.S.
    5. Thomas Register of American Manufacturers
    6. Standard Industrial Classification Manual (U.S. Government Printing Office)
    7. U.S. Industrial Outlook (U.S. Printing Office)
    8. Forbes Annual Report on American Industry
    9. INC. Magazine
    10. Wall Street Journal
    11. Dun & Bradstreet Business Information Reports
    12. Encyclopedia of Associations (Gale Research Inc.)
    13. Specific trade publications

Something worth discussing at this time, for those of you with children still at home, is how do you explain what happened to you, and even more importantly , how will this affect them. At some point the kids will be wondering,(unless you have some texting teenagers who haven't figured out your home yet, so you may want to text them) whether they will have to move, find new friends, quit soccer camp, never get that car you promised, and God forbid , wear sneakers that are less than $150.00! (I would text the clothes issue to them rather than bringing it up face to face).

I was fortunate that my "children" were 35 and 31, one married, the other independent, self-supporting, both doing well and understanding of what life can throw at you. Although I know how badly they felt for me (which by the way is not how it is supposed to be....kids worrying about parents at least not until I start wearing Depends!) it is still hard to face them with an answer to the question, "what happened, dad?" For some, you are the person they looked up to, the security blanket, the one that was the foundation and the go to person when *they* hit a wall. Will that change, they wonder? Will dad or mom, continue to be the rock, the one who says..."this too shall pass?" Can I joke with them? Should I reach out more or leave them alone? How can I help? Will we, or they, have to move?

The "why did this happen dad (mom)?" is probably harder to explain to children in a certain age range. The real young ones are not that focused on the entire dynamic and when mom or dad says "it's all OK", they have blind faith. The adult aged children hopefully have matured to the point where you can sit down and lay out the reality of the situation, your plan (when it's ready for prime time) and what part they play in the process and "journey". There must be a middle (teenage) range (I'm sure Dr. Phil has this nailed down, so I will defer) that is potentially as devastated by this life altering change–to *their* life, not necessarily *your* life.

I can only suggest you understand this situation has impact beyond you. The sad part mentioned in Chapter 1 is the almost cavalier manner in which you are told early on, "You will land on your feet." You know, that disingenuous comment, almost inherently implies it is only about you (which is probably the frame of reference that the employer comes from; you the employee, not the whole family).

Each day I was out of work, I was faced with the double edged sword. I wanted to, I needed to reach out to my family, but every time I did it was a reminder that perhaps I let them down. They never made me feel this way, it was something I put on myself. The foundation, or part of the foundation, of the family, the "stable part" of life, was changing. I cannot tell you how unhealthy this perception is. It has been reiterated

25

to me by so many of us "journeymen". Personally, I think it is by far the most gut wrenching part of the whole situation.

If you really are struggling with this aspect, my only advice is to get some help, talk to a professional (not an outplacement service, but a therapist).You cannot focus on what you have to accomplish if you are laden with guilt. Remember, you didn't create the environment that caused your release (unless it was a discharge for cause). Let me reiterate, "don't play the victim", but take necessary actions to get help. It is how you rebound after a crisis which shows your character and who you are. Your family will see that you are rising above a dilemma, handling a crisis and eventually taking control of a bad situation. An invaluable life lesson instilled by one they admire and who's doing their primary job....being a parent and positive role model. So, hang in there, get your head screwed back on, talk to those most affected, and WORK on YOUR Plan....OOOHHH, by the way that's NOT a suggestion, my friend!

Presented in Table 4 is a "Survival Plan" for the early stage of your *journey.* Consider taking some time to implement all, or at least some, of these steps.

Table 4: A 10-Step Program for Survival

Step 1: File a claim for unemployment insurance the first day after you lose your job (even if you received a severance package).

Step 2: Take a week or two to de-stress. This is one of the most stressful events you will deal with. Take a few days to decompress and have breakfast, lunch or dinner with friends. Catch up on some sleep or small projects around the house. Maybe even go visit your parents or children.

Step 3: Evaluate your financial situation. Are all your finances organized? What are your expenses per month? What expenses are fixed versus discretionary? Can you cut back on spending, even if just for the short term?

Step 4: Get started on your plan. Determine objectives and evaluate your strengths, weaknesses, areas of interest, etc. Sketch out a preliminary plan, and share with your spouse.

Step 5: Get working on your resume and cover letters. Customize both as needed for a particular opportunity or position.

Step 6: Get your networking going. This will be the most effective and probable avenue to finding a position. Introductions by a business associate or friend can help "get you in the door".

Step 7: Be prepared for interviews. Not only by preparing your comments and answers to the "most likely questions", but also by doing some interview role playing with friends or a coach. Be sure you have the proper attire available for an interview and be mindful of first impressions (you only get one shot at a first impression!)

Step 8: Invest in expanding your credentials and skills. There will be time available to take on various self-improvement, professional enhancement initiatives. For example, increase your computer skills; take courses in areas you are not as strong (e.g. accounting, marketing). Or consider taking a foreign (second) language (being bi-lingual cannot hurt!).

Step 9: Take some downtime at the end of the day and maintain your health. A clear mind and a healthy body can benefit you throughout this journey. Reading, yoga, and exercise are all good ways to quiet the mind and strengthen the body.

Step 10: Be visible. Don't isolate yourself or "disappear". Keep a positive attitude and interact. Besides being good for your overall well being, you never know where that next offer may come from!

"When we are no longer able to <u>change</u> a situation, we are challenged to change ourselves." ~**Victor Frankl**

Do We Have a Plan For You!

"Great opportunities come to all, but many do not know they have met them. The only preparation to take advantage of them is simple fidelity to watch what each day brings." ~Alfred E. Dunning

Some of us were "lucky" enough to have been given a resource known as "Outplacement Services". I am not sure what the heck "outplacement" means other than a synonym for screwed, dumped, tossed, or displaced (probably would make more sense being called Displacement Services). Or perhaps it is the English translation for "mea culpa" (for the non-Catholics, that is basically what we Catholics say as we ask for forgiveness). Anyway, it is one of those "severance" items that really makes the leadership feel good, that they "took care of one of our own" and creates a warm fuzzy feeling all the way to the top of the organization. When asked by others "did you treat them well (the discarded ones)?" The HR leader can say with confidence, "yes, we did, we gave them "outplacement services". And a quiet peace ran through the company.... how nice!

Again, using the Catholic analogy, it is like the company went to confession to ask for forgiveness for the "sin of discharge" (which is more venial than mortal but can still mess up their entrance to the pearly gates). For your penance, thou shalt give 6 months' severance (synonymous with 5 Our Father's) AND 6 months of outplacement services (which is as close to 10 Hail Mary's as it gets!). So, they feel good about their kindness and you get some resources that may be helpful, all said and done. Resources that you may not have considered accessing or you may not have otherwise financially afforded.

Outplacement services, or life management consulting, career planning counseling, whatever the term, is basically a process. The process begins with you being assigned to a "counselor". There may be 100 other fancier, more politically correct titles for the position, but at the end of the day, it's a counselor. Many of these individuals are ex HR types, business people or formerly "outplaced" individuals. Some are specialized for C suite individuals (CEO, COO, CFO, CIO, etc.), but most deal with all levels of the "severed". Their role is not to find you a job. They are not recruiters. Probably the biggest misunderstanding when someone is first introduced to this resource.

Table 5: Definition of Outplacement Services

Outplacement services is defined as "the process of facilitating a terminated employee's search for a new job, by provision of professional services, such as counseling, paid for by the former employer." (The American Heritage Dictionary of the American Language). Or as noted on the website of U.S. Legal Inc.: "Outplacement is a group of services given to displaced employees that provides them with support or assistance in making the career transition. Outplacement programs may be offered on a voluntary basis to personnel being terminated, those who are encouraged to take early retirement, as well as those who remain with the organization. Outplacement services may be offered because of ethical concerns for displaced workers, to reduce the stress- level of managers involved in layoffs, to maintain the morale of remaining employees, to preserve the company's reputation as a good corporate citizen, and other reasons. Outplacement may include, among others, the following services:

- Asset Analysis/Career Assessment
- One-on-One Counseling
- Personal Marketing Strategies

- Communication and Self Presentation Enhancement
- Follow-up Support

Recruiters get paid to find you a new position. They're paid by the company looking to fill a position. Nothing wrong with these folks, other than they want to "fill a position", not necessarily with *you*, but with *someone*. They are paid either on retainer or by percent of the new hires compensation.

Table 6: Key Points Related to Recruiters/Search Firms
<u>Retained</u> Search Firms:
- hired by companies to identify qualified candidates, and are on an exclusive basis with the company
- generalists, or boutique firms specializing in an industry or position (e.g.CFO)
- selective about candidates and present a very "short list" to the client (company), typically 3-4 candidates
- assess and screen candidates to the degree negotiated with client
- are about satisfying the needs of the client, which is the company, and do not work on your behalf
- charge client 30-35% of candidates first year salary; some work on straight flat rate

<u>Contingent</u> Search Firms:
- are not technically hired by the company but if their candidate is selected, will receive compensation
- are more specialist then generalist
- receive 15-30% of the candidates first year salary if candidate is placed
- Believe the more resumes and candidates, the better; they send many resumes to the same company
- are not exclusive to client and certainly not to the one seeking a job

- may try to "place" candidate in any open position, as opposed to best scenario for candidate

Outplacement counselors are there to "prepare you" to find a job, or "your new life's path". They will lead you through a process and point the way to resources which you can access on your journey. They are like a video game wizard ...as you move through your journey and advance in the levels (those of you who have started playing games to kill some time know EXACTLY what I mean!), you will acquire items and "powers" (invisibility, flight, weapons, life sustaining nourishment, immortality...OK back to the point!), which will aid you on your quest... your quest to "Land on Your Feet".

First, you will meet the chosen one–your proposed counselor. He or she will sit down with you for an hour or so to evaluate your situation, including your emotional readiness, and the "fit" of working together. There may be some "pre-meeting paperwork" to fill out, but trust me, you haven't seen anything yet! In some cases you may meet a number of counselors and then be asked to "choose". You will hear how, "you must move on", "let this go", "look to the future", "work on your plan" and my favorite, "it is not IF you will land on your feet, it is WHEN". There is certainly an aspect of motivational encouragement. Although, probably not the stuff you want to hear right after getting the crap kicked out of you.

In fact, as many have confirmed, at that first session you really don't listen to what is being said, you hear a voice, like the voice of the teacher in Charlie Brown movies, the person you never see but can hear "waw, waw, waw, waw, waw!" You can imagine that the words are meaningful, but you are still thinking "where am I, is this really happening?" "Who are you?" "Did you really just say..."*let it go*?" and "*this is an opportunity*?!"

After your first meeting you will probably be given some materials... well let's say "lots of materials". You will take one or more "who are you?" tests such as the Myers Briggs or DISC. You may even go beyond those to answering all kinds of #2 pencil questions (you remember those?

ONLY use #2 pencils. I always felt bad for the #3 pencil salesman who was probably *"outplaced"*).

I love those Myers Briggs tests. I must have done those three or four times in my life. And oddly enough I come out the same every time. I think I was an ESPN (someone who likes sports). When the results were back, the counselor gave me about a 50 page document that had an explanation of my strengths, weaknesses, preferences, attitudes, and about 10 different graphs on which attributes companies are looking for, and more. I listened for almost two hours about all that I can do and how to interpret this report, what the graphs meant, how I compared to norm, my red zones, my green zones, my yellow zones. And I am thinking, for the love of God, someone else totally screwed up this company, fell asleep at the wheel, overreacted or didn't react to the marketplace, panicked, WHATEVER, and I am undergoing tests to see if I can be more effective? What is wrong with this picture? Here's a thought... give these tests to the people who created the apparent need to outplace people. Maybe *their* "yellows" should be worked on.

If you can set your bitterness aside, some of the information from these tests can be beneficial. Whether you are willing to accept the "data" is up to you–especially if you have been in the workforce for 30 plus years, and, as an employee, had recently completed a series of these behavioral and analytical tests. For me, about 3 years before being severed, my results suggested I was "someone with conceptual and operational leadership abilities *who has the ability to rise within the organization*"! Imagine that!

Another benefit of the outplacement service is the provocation to get you to write your resume–THE resume–the one that separates you from all others, the one that at the end of the day looks just like all the others since they are getting the same advice. I was counseled to take my time and really put thought into this resume and not to get it out until it was ready for prime time. Sounded like good advice until I realized that you could be in rewrite iterations for decades and that no matter what you wrote, what format you used, every "expert" has a different opinion. I sent my first draft (although I considered it pretty well complete) to my counselor as well as others in the HR or recruitment profession. Every one of them had a different spin on how to make this THE resume. After so many revisions I finally said…OOOHHH I need to get this thing out! I need people to get a basic idea of what I have done and more importantly, what I can do for them.

Gotta tell you, I received immediate reaction and interest. I continued getting it circulated through my network and beyond. So my advice is: don't search for the Holy Grail version of your resume. Don't produce a 5th grade version either. There are plenty of resources that will illustrate a variety of ways to prepare the document. Check them out, select one, write it, have someone proof it and get it out there.

There are many resume writing services that are available to you. If you are engaged with an Outplacement service they will certainly assist you. If not, surf the web and you will see a multitude of options or visit your local Barnes and Noble for a "How to" book. There are also potential local resources which you may access through organizations such as SCORE, Chamber of Commerce, private individuals (check local advertising), or smaller consulting firms (specializing in Coaching and Counseling). Formats vary and you would need to select a style and format that suits your needs. All styles include:

Table 7: Resume Highlights
- Heading: includes name, address, e-mail address, telephone, fax and credentials (CPA, MD).
- Profile Statement: description of who you are (your thirty second commercial). including background, experience, strengths, contributions and level of position sought.
- Professional Experience: titles, company information, employment years, brief job duties, elaborate on accomplishments.
- Educational Background: educational institutions, degree, dates, special training (such as leadership institutes), proficiency in additional languages, certificates, and accreditations or recognition.
- Affiliations/Community Involvement: professional af-

filiations, board participation, community volunteerism, military duty,

- Personal Interests: hobbies, pastimes, non-work related expertise (e.g. automotive skills).

Beyond the self-analysis phase and the resume writing, the services offered by the outplacement firm can create additional value. The counselor will suggest that you use the social media avenues to "get the message out". Actually this surprised me. I didn't think for a senior executive position that LinkedIn, Twitter or Facebook would be the avenue to take. After reading many articles and hearing recruiters recommend this approach, I decided it was time to try and join the "connected" world. Obviously you can go on line and learn how to use LinkedIn and the others, however, I will forewarn you to be prepared for "connections"...*everyday*! I didn't say job offers, I said *connections*. You will be asked every day by someone to "join their network". This can be extremely frustrating as you start getting e-mails mostly from others looking for work or just wanting to expand their personal network. So, if you are looking to build your primary and secondary network, or feel disconnected right after being discharged, this may be something to consider (more on this in Chapter 7).

The overall message of this chapter is the outplacement center may be of assistance even if by just giving you access to social media educational seminars (or webinars...get with the program!). If you don't have an office set up in your home or a quiet area with privacy, then one excellent feature of most outplace operations is that you are given "shared" cubicle space. Sounds harsh, "shared cubicle space", and for many that is what we began our careers in (a kind of déjà vu). If you need a professional environment to do your research and contacting, or are not disciplined enough to work at home and stay away from watching Fox News, CNN, MSNBC, or even Regis or Oprah then leaving to "go to work" can be a huge asset. The center will have the basic office supplies, means to communicate with the outside world (telephone, fax, internet), and in some cases, administrative support. If your company purchased what I will call the "total cleansing–sainthood package", you may also get business cards, letterhead, mail service, typing, and message taking.

The other benefit of having a place to go is you will meet others who are also taking the journey. The theory is that you can all exchange prospects and leads as you sit around the camp fire exchanging stories. This is the perfect world, everyone exchanging openly and handing leads to one another. Not sure how much that really happens in this economy with the shortage of jobs, but any "nugget" you get is a "good nugget" (this was first uttered during the gold rush).

What I will caution, however, is that you do not get caught up in the "who got screwed worse" conversations, or "things just can't get any worse". Remember there will be many individuals in the same boat, looking for the same paddles, and telling the same "old sea" stories. If you are impressionable, or still in the extreme venting stage, I would recommend caution when entering the cubicle.

Another feature of the outplacement experience is gaining access to "how to" experts, that are brought in as guest speakers (not the ones from Home Depot or Lowes) . Here is where the nugget gathering can increase. You may have access to financial planners, estate planners, recruiters, PR professionals, social media experts, and a litany of "helpful hints" type people. Quite frankly, I picked up a few nuggets along the way and I bet you would too. If you have this opportunity, I urge you to consider taking it. In the worst case it may spur you to getting back in touch with the advisors you may not have talked to in years (your attorney, banker, estate planner, and accountant). So again, keeping in mind that the primary goal of the outplacement service is to help 'nudge you along', give you access to tools that can help, and give you some exposure to topical experts, this is not such a bad deal.

I will tell you that I have heard many instances where individuals, middle and senior leaders, have said to me, "I wish the company had given me the dollars they spent on the outplacement firm. I could have accomplished what they do without their guidance, and the cash would have been very helpful." To be fair, there are also many who have mentioned that the outplacement was a great help.

There are organized "support" meetings which the center will arrange; usually a group in your industry (e.g. healthcare, banking, manufacturing), or your profession (e.g. finance, marketing, information systems). These can be helpful as much as any support group can be. It is a personal choice but I would suggest at least trying one to see if it brings value to you emotionally or with respect to market reconnaissance or job leads.

Listed in Table 8 are the types of services which can be available to you. For the most part, they are purchased by the company, but you can self pay for a menu of services at many firms, particularly local, smaller companies. You can Google "outplacement services" and find listings for national, regional and local firms.

Table 8: Outplacement Services
- One on one career transition counseling
- Resume preparation assistance
- Cover Letter preparation assistance
- Interviewing consultation and practice sessions
- Video recording and assessment of interviewing skills
- Job profile analysis
- Evaluation of strengths, weaknesses and areas of interest
- Matching of personal profiles and career options
- Resume posting or interactive database
- Access and advice related to executive recruiters
- Opportunities to network
- Presentations on key job search elements
- Access to industry and recruitment experts
- Work station availability
- Clerical support, use of email, and telephone coverage
- Personalized salary market analysis
- Evaluation of progress and plan of action

Another aspect of the "outplaced" world I find fascinating is the concept of being FORTUNATE. You may have been told, "This is a new beginning, a new chance to start again, to really assess what you want to do for the rest of your life" and "that you are so fortunate". Well, not exactly the perspective that came to mind. I keep coming back to "I *was* doing what I wanted to do until retirement". Perhaps this would be a *fortunate* thing...in about 10 years when I turn 65 and find myself ready for that "new life".

Sure, when retired, everyone wants to run a surfboard shop in Maui, or, open that pizza shop they dreamed of since eating that first slice of heaven. (Being an Italian-American from Brooklyn, guess which was my dream?!) But, to suggest that being placed in an unemployed position, with or without severance, is the PERFECT time to pursue your life's ambition is at best disingenuous or as they say in marketing circles, "putting lipstick on a pig".

For the preponderance of those I have encountered along their "journey", those with mortgages, college tuition, health care related bills, car payments and other financial commitments (sandwich generation), this concept of cultivating a new career, living the dream, starting anew, is not Plan A. Taking care of their responsibilities, reducing impact on the quality of their life, keeping the family together and having some degree of peace of mind, is Plan A. Venturing into a brave new world, opening up that risky business or starting in a new field or profession is at Best, Plan B or C while we are in the midst of the worst recession (2009-2010) since the Great One and some economists are predicting another "Great One" in 2011-2012. Not only are we faced with the typical burdens of being in mid-life, but now we need to compete for positions that are few and probably miles from home. We are sandwiched between the needs (emotional and financial) of our children (maybe grandchildren) and assisting in the care of aged parents.

Arguably for some, those that are truly miserable every day and dying a slow death (like Willy Lowman from death of a Salesman), this may be the wakeup call needed. It may even lead to a longer, less stressful life. But for the many, I would say the vast majority; this is not the solution to life's humdrum, mundane, and painful 10-12 hours per day. In fact, the stress level for those that are placed into this situation, particularly in their 50's, is higher as they become fearful and concerned about the next few years. I often wonder if the mantra "this is a chance to start again, live your dream, and improve your quality of life", isn't really to help those responsible for your situation, or those trying to help you "land" (outplacement counselor) feel better. Friends may use that approach to try to ease your pain, or be supportive, or upbeat. I have told many of my closest friends that I appreciate what you are trying to do, but make no mistake about it, until you have experienced what we are going through, the joy of "a new beginning" is not what is going through our minds.

What happens, and this may be what you are experiencing, is that you "have" to focus on this positive spin and force yourself to adapt to the situation. Some may land in a position that is a clone of their former job. I hope so and wish them well. I am sure they have learned from this experience and may take that leap of faith sometime in the future and open that surfing shop at the beach. But the reality is; most will not. Recognizing that options may be different than you hoped for, this MAY be the best time to go for that change of life (not the one with the hot flashes, which by the way, my wife is convinced also happens to men!). You convince yourself that creative options to moving on may have to be explored. So I ask, is this really taking the opportunity of a life time, or is it just plain survival? Only you know the answer.

I will say that to keep your sanity, and perhaps as you look for the "similar" job, explore other avenues. You will have time to do so. For example, if you believe that being bilingual is something you always aspired to, and it may give you an advantage in the job market, then spend time learning a new language. If you always thought you wanted to own and run your own business, research what it takes to do so. Spend time at SCORE, or your local Chamber of Commerce. You can even take courses on line or attend local community colleges to enhance not only your portfolio, but to give you exposure and insight into alternative careers paths. You can use the time productively or you can watch Regis and Kelly. Your search will more than likely take time. And, especially for those who are high performers, you will be frustrated by the amount of "downtime" or "unproductive time. Many will tell you to "relax a bit" and "take some time for yourself". I agree with that to a certain extent. Might as well use some of this diversion time to catch your breath (like a sabbatical for a teacher…except they can go right back to the same job when it's over).

At the outset, I was a networking machine (see next chapter), and filled each hour with some activity that moved the ball up the court (or puck up the ice for our Canadian friends). I found it extremely hard to just plan a couple of hours per day for the "search" and the rest of the time for personal reflection and "chill" time (as the kids say). But as time goes on you will realize that *balance* is really the key. You will need to try and balance all aspects of the productive time (networking, writing, e-mailing, conference calls, and research) and the "downtime". Don't forget this is an extremely stressful time. You will not only be dealing with the stress that comes from internalizing the situation (what did I do, how could the outcome be different, what will I be doing in the future, is this the end of my professional life?) but the external stressors such as dealing with the impact on your family, answering the same questions over and over again from friends and colleagues, dealing with rejection ("sorry, no position available") , and analyzing what to do next (that one is so hard for a high performer). So, you will need downtime if for no other reason than to clear your thoughts and maintain your health.

I highly recommend working hard at finding that next opportunity, but accomplish other things along the way. This "ride" may be a long one. It would be a shame to look back and say, "Where did the time go"? "I coulda, woulda, shoulda, been able to do this and that in that time" Me? I am still trying to lose those 20 pounds I swore I would by the time I landed–2 pounds down, 18 to go!

One thing I did do since day one of my "journey" was to maintain my daily Outlook Calendar. It forced me to refrain from letting the entire day slip away. It kept me grounded in the need to meet (and even exceed!) expectations and it forced me to plan. Yes, some of my entries were, "pick up the dry cleaning, cut the grass, and call my children, but keeping a calendar and daily/weekly "to do list" had been instrumental in keeping me grounded, focused on what needed to be done and allowed me to "plan" the downtime which I needed to refresh without losing the entire day, or week, or month. If you have not begun doing this, try it for a week. Get passed the fact that your calendar used to have some higher level appointments and use this tool to help stay the course on your journey. It may also prove to be positive when you hit one of those walls and you wonder; "what have I been doing?" You can go back and look and see if you have to rethink your strategy, time utilization, and your next steps. Hopefully the calendar will reinforce that you are out there trying to make it happen. But, if it shows otherwise, then it's time to take some personal responsibility and address the need to straighten yourself out.

One of the most important aspects of getting through this process is staying organized and focused. You will want to stay abreast on a great deal of information as well as plan your day so as to not fall into bad habits. Utilize your Outlook Calendar, not only noting appointments, but compile your "to do list", schedule tasks and record completed items. It can also be used to record key information which you are tracking or intend to research. In conjunction with utilizing Outlook, you should also maintain a file folder, or multiple file folders, (a filing system per se) to organize information and future opportunities (e.g. market research, social media, job opportunities and interviews, etc).

Table 9: Staying Focused and Organized
Key areas of information to track include the following:
- Contacts
- Notes from telephone conversations
- Market research information
- Reference letters
- Correspondences (intro letters, responses to ads, thank you notes)
- Magazine articles
- Potential Employers
- Former employer documents
- Your business expenses (don't forget to keep track of these!)
- Prospects folders
- Social Media activity

Whether the "fortunate aspect" of this situation is something you embrace or not, it may be the perspective you need to survive and move forward. You don't have to drink the "Opportunity Kool-Aid", but you do need to try and turn lemons into lemonade.

"When one door closes, another opens. But we often look so long and so regretfully upon the closed door that we do not see which has opened for us." ~Alexander Graham Bell

"Hello, My Name is Bob."
"Hi Bob!"

"Things may come to those that wait, but only the things left by those who hustle." ~Abraham Lincoln

There is a classic scene in just about every movie or TV show that employs any kind of support group. It is the scene where the new member of the group stands up and says, "My name is Bob", and before he can continue his introductory remarks, the group shouts in a harmonic, melodic rhythm, "Hi Bob". This encounter is the perfect metaphor for what this chapter will address–the lifeline of being on the journey–NETWORKING. The single best way to find your next job or lead for a new venture is through a contact, someone you know, or via the concept of "degrees" of connection (recall the game "Six Degrees of Kevin Bacon" noted in the insert). Thus, the network you have will be critical to your success in "landing".

SIX DEGREES of KEVIN BACON

A trivia game based on the concept of the small world phenomenon and rests on the assumption that any individual can be linked through his or her film roles to actor Kevin Bacon within six steps. The name of the game is a pun on the philosophical "Six Degrees of Separation" theory. This game was developed by three college friends who went to Albright College (Reading, PA). They first appeared on the Jon Stewart show on MTV (Jon's old show—not "The Daily Show"). It is based on the theory that Kevin Bacon is the center of the entertainment universe, and that any actor or actress can be linked back to him within six degrees (connections). Variations on this game are based on the theory that almost anyone in the world can be linked to anyone else in the world by six or seven degrees. Example: Linking Bela Lugosi to Kevin Bacon on three degrees: 1. Bela Lugosi was in "Abbott and Costello Meet Frankenstein" (1948) with Vincent Price. 2. Vincent Price was in "The Raven" (1963) with Jack Nicholson. 3. Jack Nicholson was in "A Few Good Men" (1992) with Kevin Bacon.

Networking is defined as "the exchange of information or services among individuals, groups, or institutions". Networking is a process of building and maintaining relationships that are mutually beneficial. Networking can be done anyplace, anytime and whenever an opportunity arises. It involves requesting information and asking for advice and for leads. Although it is not something that comes easily to everyone, it is absolutely a critical part of the job finding process. It is estimated that 70% of those seeking new jobs find their positions through contacts (their network). It must be continually worked at and should be started immediately in the job finding process. Develop a list of contacts from the various sources listed in Table 10.

Table 10: Contact Categories
- Family/ friends / neighbors
- Former classmates and alumni of educational institutions
- Business associates
- Local legislatures/politicians
- Bankers/lawyers/CPA's
- Small Business Owners
- Professional Associations
- Chamber of Commerce associates
- Church members and clergy
- Current and former employees
- Current and former employers

- Acquaintances at attended seminars and conferences
- Business association members (Rotary, Lion's Club, Kiwanis, etc.)
- Board member associates
- Past clients, vendors, consultants and sales professionals
- Social media contacts (LinkedIn, facebook, Twitter, etc)
- Parents of children's friends
- Spouses contacts and business associates
- Recruiters
- Personal coaches or counselors

As soon as possible upon receiving the news, you should begin compiling a list of everyone you know–yes I said *everyone* you know. This list should not only be the obvious cast of characters, such as family, friends, long time business contacts, members of the church or associations you belong too, neighbors, etc. You will need to S-T-R-E-T-C-H your thinking and be creative. Look through your rolodex (it's the black box next to the eight track); consider individuals you may have met (even if briefly) at trade shows, conferences, or seminars (look for the attendees list); consider local leaders who you may have been introduced to over time, or board members that you have volunteered with. Use the list in Table 10 to jog your memory about categories of contacts to consider.

After you compile your contact list, but before you pick up the telephone or sit down at your computer, you'll want to script your message. One approach is to develop what is referred to as your "elevator speech" (named so because of the ups and downs of this process!) This is your equivalent of a 30 second commercial and assumes that you have someone's attention for that brief amount of time (after which they start to glaze over or give you the fake "I'm paying attention head bob" like you may give your spouse or vice versa). An elevator speech is a short 30 second (150 words) sound bite that succinctly and in a memorable manner, introduces you , describes who you are , what you can offer, what problems you can solve, what contributions you can make and what the listener should do after hearing about you. Elevator speeches are brief and prepare you for those unexpected encounters where you only have a short period of time to make and leave an impression. Although commonly called elevator speeches, they can be used at any chance encounter (such as at a seminar, business association event, at a club meeting, etc). An effective speech should:

1. Be short and sweet
2. Use everyday language
3. Create a visual image of you by the listener
4. Describe your abilities in an action oriented manner

Include a "hook", something to peak interest and suggest action by the listener. In essence it communicates who you are, what you are looking for and how you can benefit a company. Outplacement counselors and personal coaches can assist in preparing the speech. You can also find resources on the internet. This sounds like such a simple task, developing a 30 second speech about a subject which you should be an expert in–you. But, believe me, this may be one of the more difficult tasks I am recommending. This has to sum you up, be interesting and leave them asking for more. Condensing who you are in a few sentences is a monumental task. Try it and see if I am wrong.

Table 11 presents two elevator speech examples. You don't have to memorize your speech verbatim or read from a teleprompter or cue cards, but you should cover the main message while hitting the highlights.

Table 11: Sample Elevator Speeches
SAMPLE #1:

"Hello, my name is John Smith. I've had many years experience in the software design industry. During my years in this business I have been fortunate to work for progressive companies that support innovation and entrepreneurial style. This suits well with what excites and motivates me. I have focused my talents on designing systems that are replacements for the burdensome legacy systems found in many organizations. I have worked with the latest technologies, continually strive for staying ahead of the

design curve and am committed to expanding my knowledge and exposure to new ideas which will benefit my company. I work extremely well in a team setting and have been characterized as a leader on several projects. I think strategically but am skilled at execution. I can make a significant impact in an organization if they are leading edge, empower their leaders and expect objectives to be exceeded. Can I set up a time to meet and discuss how my skills can benefit your company? Or do you know anyone else who may be looking for such qualities in a leader?"

SAMPLE #2:

"Hi, my name is Maria Rodriguez. I am a sales professional with 15 years experience in direct sales in the manufacturing industry. Besides having a background in sales, starting at the customer support level, I have advanced to the position of Regional VP, responsible for 25 sales individuals for a Fortune 500 company. My experience also includes development of sales training programs and mentoring the less experienced staff as they grow with the company. I am not only a self starter but consider myself to have an entrepreneurial attitude and focus. Although I have focused recently in the sale of equipment, my skills are adaptable to other products and services. I am goal oriented and strive to exceed the objectives set. My degree in marketing has helped me understand the expectations of the client and allows me to communicate effectively with the marketing team in the organization which is a critical relationship for success. If your company wants to grow and is looking for a sales executive that can develop strategy and implement a direct sales function, I would welcome the opportunity to discuss a position with your company and how I can help you achieve your goals. Or if you are aware of a business associate who may be interested in my abilities, I would appreciate an introduction or their contact information."

You will then need to translate the "speech" into a communication piece which can be sent via a variety of "mailing" medium. The first of which will be the more traditional e-mail approach. Now, there are two versions to this, what I will call the "mass mailing approach" and the "contact specific method". The mass mailing is basically the use of a generic e-mail that introduces your situation, presents your elevator speech and is not personalized more than the addressing of the e-mail. This approach is somewhat less personal but can communicate to numerous people at one time. You may modify this approach by grouping contacts (such as friends, family, business associates, acquaintances) and tailoring your message to fit the audience.

Using the more personal approach can be very positive strategically but more time consuming. In this method you are making a personal connection with the contact. You can use personal experiences, reference shared accomplishments, note past interactions, and perhaps use a more relaxed tone. You want to be certain though, not to stray from the message. Stay on point even if personalizing. Don't become verbose, cute or take a liberty with a close contact and drift into venting. Remember, you want this individual to understand your availability, what your value will be to a business.

The last element is very important. The contact needs to know what they might be able to do for you. What you are asking of them. Do you want them to forward information to their business associates, are you asking if they have a job available, are you asking for them to critique your resume (if attached)? All too often, the contact is left, after reading the communication, without a clear "call to action". This becomes obvious when you receive a response such as "sorry to hear this, thanks for letting me know". If that is all you receive then you probably missed the mark.

Before discussing the other communication vehicles which you should employ (the social media phenomena), the readiness of your resume is a major component of the initial communication. There can be two schools of thought on this issue. The more common position is that before any communication goes out, your resume needs to be included. I generally agree with that. The only caveat is that if you are struggling with the format or as mentioned in an earlier chapter, being advised to revise the resume "ad nauseam", you may have people out there wondering about your situation and why they haven't heard from you. Or you may miss opportunities. The experts will be adamant about holding off until your resume is spot on. In making certain contacts, like applying for a position, or introducing yourself to a recruiter, I concur. But, I think a two-step approach with the primary contacts (family, friends, and longtime business associates) can be done. The first communication explains your current status, your 30 second commercial, a reference to the "planning" which you are engaged in, and that your resume will be sent to them soon.

You then have the opportunity to contact them a second time, update your status and include your resume. Only you can determine which contacts will be responsive to the two step approach without feeling bothered. I will tell you that the two-step worked very well for me and for several others I have spoken to. It may not be for everyone, but to overlook its merits can cause you to miss an opportunity.

Something you will definitely want to do is keep track of your contacting effort. If you are a sales professional you are probably used to logging contact calls on a software package, such as ACT or Goldmine. If you have access to such a program, that would be excellent. But for the rest of us, a simple pen and pad will do (as dad used to say...don't make everything so damn complicated). You will want to maintain a record of who you called, or e-mailed, what your purpose or "ask" was (a possible contact name, a time to meet, a time to call, etc), if the individual responded, and if so, how. The beauty of having a software program is that it can search the "open" contacts faster than your manual filing. Coding by hand requires having to do a few "look backs". For those of us who relied heavily on an administrative assistant for so many years, you will get a very profound appreciation for how they kept you organized. If you haven't done so by now, even though you are gone, you should send them flowers with a thank you note!

The record keeping will prevent you from making oversights that would detract from the professional image you need to project. It certainly has prevented me from sending duplicate resumes as well as an "introduction letter" followed by another introductory letter a week later (wouldn't that be impressive!). It also allows you to reference previous conversations or e-mails and therefore projects the image you are organized and focused.

Noted in Table 12 is a simple form. For those who are thoroughly impressed with yourself and your innate ability to maintain a huge amount of data, keep in mind that you will be on an emotional roller coaster with days that are not as they used to be. There was order and continuity during your day (even the hectic days). Things have changed and committing "phone calls and e-mails" to memory, especially at this volume (if you are working your network) is not what you were used to doing or want to start doing.

Table 12: Sample Tracking Log

Date	Contact	Call/Email	Responded	Action	Comments

Start out by accepting that using tools appearing rudimentary for someone of your stature and former position in life will be helpful in getting you back in the game. Between your contact notes and your daily calendar, you will become a networking guru. For those who have been project leaders, consider yourself as "The Project". This is project management 101.

In addition to the need to make contact via phone or e-mail, there are other forms of networking which are critical. The first is "old school" (as the kids say), and involves becoming, or staying active in the local Chamber of Commerce, Rotary, Professional Associations, and other means of community service. Basically, GET OUT THERE! Be VISIBLE and OUT IN FRONT! The obvious reason is to increase your contact base and to tell "your story". Another reason, especially if you are in a small community and have been active in the community during your career, is to let everyone know, *"this is not the end, but the beginning. Yes, it sucks, but I can adapt and will adjust*". I will not place my tail between my legs and hide. This will take more intestinal fortitude than you can imagine. You will have to check your ego at the door and be confident enough to tell people, some who you have known for years, face to face, that you are no longer with XYZ, and (without gritting your teeth) you are on a new "journey". You state that you are in the midst of developing your plan for the future and when the time is right you would like to have an opportunity to share it with them. Or if you have the plan in place, proceed to share.

I have spoken to so many individuals (particularly the middle aged 50-60 men....geez I guess that's me...middle aged!) who have found it so difficult to put themselves in the public setting where they have to explain they are "available for work". One of my hardest moments was to serve as master of ceremonies at the Local YMCA annual meeting (I was chairperson of the organization at that time) and keep an "upper lip" after being "let go" from my senior position only one week earlier. For the most part the audience was filled with local captains of industry, benefactors of the YMCA and even local legislatures. Most may not yet have heard of my situation. I was very apprehensive about leading the meeting, especially since I knew I was receiving accolades for my leadership of the YMCA Board through a major reorganization and capital campaign. What to do?

A couple of days prior to the meeting, I had the opportunity to interact with another executive who had been "let go" from a major organization in our region. She shared her personal story with me. Her advice was that this would be my "moment of truth". All eyes would be on how I handled myself, as a leader, during my personal crisis. She also reminded me that this meeting was not about me but the accomplishments of the organization. It could be a defining moment and should be looked at as an opportunity, and not a time for fear, embarrassment or shame.

I found that advice very helpful and did what I had to do. It was a defining moment for me. These do not come along all the time, so embrace them. Attack them rather than recoiling and wallowing in self pity. Carpe Diem, (seize the day), "man up", strap them on, whatever works for you! But don't run and hide.

Another communication method gaining huge acceptance is social media. I'm not going to try to dazzle you with my brilliance in utilizing social media as a means for networking. In fact, as I am writing this I am still trying to figure it all out. Hopefully my 10 year old niece can steer me straight! (How embarrassing is that?!)

I was shocked by the comments I heard from a number of outplacement professionals, recruiters, HR specialists, and others (even the middle aged group!) about the value of using social media. I am referring to LinkedIn, Facebook, Twitter, and even your own personal websites, mine are: youwilllandonyourfeet.com and rennaconsulting.net. The first thing my counselor told me was "get on LinkedIn". My immediate and sincere response was "Link *Who*?" Yes I am one of the millions of "50 plus-ers" that have almost mastered the basics of e-mail, and actually know how to text by cell phone (I know—impressive—but if I want to talk to my children, who by the way are in their thirties, this is the only way—I even text them on their phone to say *"answer your damn phone, I know you have it, your texting!"*).

"Social media" is an umbrella term which defines the various activities that integrate technology, social interaction, and the construction of words and pictures. This interaction and the manner in which information is presented, depends on the varied perspectives and "building" of shared meaning, as people share their stories, and understanding. Social media marketing has three important aspects according to the Internet Advertising Bureau social media council:

- Creates buzz or noteworthy events, videos, tweets or blogs that attract attention and become viral in nature (spreads quickly and exponentially).
- Builds ways for individuals, or businesses, to self promote using numerous internet sites.
- Is based on individual conversations and participation rather than organizational control of a message.

As I started to dabble with this "new fangled" thing (I felt like Jethro from the Beverly Hillbillies), I realized the enormous power of this tool. I discovered if I became a part of the network, I could be linked to 291,000 people through only my first and second tier contacts! I immediately placed my resume on the site and started to add a couple of contacts. Now, every day I am being asked to "join my network". At first, I took the position "leave me alone for heaven sake", "I haven't seen you in 20 years—or I'm not sure who you are". That was a pretty Neanderthal way to approach this powerful tool.

Although I am still not advanced as much as I would like to be (probably spending more time on this book!), I do know how to reach out and touch someone (figuratively of course!). The benefit is being able to see who is connecting to whom. If there is a person that may be of interest contacting, you can get back to your primary contact and ask for an introduction, or you can go directly to the person. There is also grouping of like contacts (classmates, professional associations, specific business leaders, etc).

Table 13: Optimizing the Use of LinkedIn

The following are tips to enhance the use of LinkedIn:

- Include a Photo: make it a current professional looking headshot
- Build Your Network: 50-100 "connections" suggests you have solid connections, whereas over 500 suggests that you will connect to anyone
- Keep your profile fresh: add capabilities and interests
- Optimize your profile: consider your full resume and a link to your portfolio and use relevant keywords
- Seek recommendations: ask for recommendations from individuals who know you and whose recommendation will be helpful
- Use the Group function: this will expand your reach and will support your business image

I will not venture to touch upon all aspects of these networking tools since by the time you read this book, there will likely be additional expansion into social media opportunities, but I will leave you with these thoughts:

- Search out the social media tools
- Consider taking a seminar or course in them EARLY on in your search
- Be careful not to become overzealous, select your contacts and the groups with a purpose in mind, otherwise, you will be inundated with messages that create no value
- Be wary to separate personal and professional information (if you want to let everyone know what you are doing each day.... develop a personal blog). You are trying to find a professional "landing" not create a reality show!

There are numerous books and internet sites that can help you get started in social media networking. I encourage you to consider researching and selecting one that can educate you on the power of this tool. As a starting point, Table 14 notes the Do's and Don'ts of social media networking. Table 15 offers a select list of business related social media networking websites.

Table 14: Do's and Don'ts of Social Media
Do's:
- Treat as an important business initiative. Define your target audience and determine your approach and objectives in networking
- Listen and learn for a few weeks before engaging and responding
- Keep the content interesting and reflective of your personality.
- Be authentic
- Engage in a "two-way" conversation, don't try to control the conversation; build trust
- Be wary of time sensitive content; focus more on timeless content

- People will choose to listen, so add value; give them a reason to stay engaged
- "Listen" in on conversations and use alerts, such as Google Alerts
- Be patient and composed and avoid attacks or defensive content
- Be open to learning from your audience

Don'ts:
- Don't mix personal and business accounts and content
- Don't be negative; emphasize your strengths and value
- Don't get started and then forget it; once started stay interactive
- Don't be compelled to disclose everything; be open and honest, but use discretion
- Don't be a generalist; be a content expert and stand out; focus on a topic
- Don't overwhelm with your information; be succinct

Table 15: List of Select Business Social Networking Websites

Biznik	Community of entrepreneurs and small businesses
Cmypitch.com	Business website for UK entrepreneurs to get quotes/advice
Cofoundr	Community of entrepreneurs involved with new ventures
E.factor	Online community and marketplace for entrepreneurs
Ecademy	Business network for creating contacts and sharing knowledge
Entrepreneur Connect	Community by Entrepreneur.com for networking
Fast Pitch	Network where professionals can market their business

Focus	Community focused on business and IT professionals
JASEzone	Community to find clients or business partners
LinkedIn	Network for introduction and collaboration with others
PartnerUp	Community for small business owners and entrepreneurs
PerfectBusiness	Network of entrepreneurs, investors and business experts
Plaxo	Enhanced address book tool for networking
Ryze	Organized by interests, location and current and past employers
StartUpNation	Community for entrepreneurs and aspiring business owners
Upspring	Site for promotion and social networking
XING	European business network
Young Entrepreneur	Site for entrepreneurs and small business owners

There is one other networking tool, or perhaps better stated, an avenue for visibility, that may be worth considering; the submission of articles to publications. You have a great deal of experience in "something". If you have any interest or ability in writing, this is an excellent way to stay in front of the business community and illustrate your knowledge, expertise and value you may bring to an organization. If you move on to consulting (Chapter 10), this can be an excellent means to prospect for potential clients.

Selecting the right publications will also be key. Consider whether you want to write for your local market or reach a regional or national audience. For example, if you prefer to stay in your local area, you may want to consider the Chamber of Commerce publication(s), newspapers, local college and university newsletters and area networking groups and business associations (such as Rotary). There are industry specific magazines and general publications (a variety of topics such as business, art, health, etc.) You can contact the publication through their website or e-mail addresses that are typically located in the publications. You can ask for the "contributing writers" process. Doesn't hurt to ask…and you may find a hidden talent and a new career!

Another possibility is to develop a seminar, course or presentation which you can offer through the Chamber of Commerce, a local college, or via a networking group. You can either charge a fee (if you can get it) or present for free and gain visibility and potential leads. Research the number and types of classes and seminars offered in your area and endeavor to fill a gap. This could produce income, notoriety as a content expert, and lead to consulting work or a job offer. Furthermore, it keeps you viable and visible during your search.

The extension of this option would be to consider teaching at a local college or university as an adjunct professor. You would need to ascertain the criteria to do so, but in most cases it requires a post graduate degree in your area of expertise. It is all about networking, visibility and relationship building. If you are an introvert, you may want to start hanging around some extroverts and pick up a few tips!

TABLE 16: Networking Essentials, Be:
- GENUINE: build trust and display integrity by being authentic.
- CLEAR: differentiate yourself by having clear and articulated goals.
- POSITIVE: display positivity and smile, being mindful that attitude is everything.
- PERSONABLE: networking is a "personal" business, make others comfortable with you.
- PROFESSIONAL: always project a professional demeanor; including implementing timely and effective follow through.
- VISIBLE: Attend as many events and group meetings that align with your career objectives and position expectations.

- PREPARED: have your "elevator speech" at the ready, know your potential audience and be brief, do not over sell.
- ENGAGING: be a good listener, enthusiastic conversationalist and use open ended questions to open up discussion.
- FOCUSED: have a networking strategy and use your time and money effectively.
- HELPFUL: help others who have helped you, and become a volunteer, give back to your community.
- RESOURCEFUL: participate in activities, write articles (or papers), do speaking engagements as an opportunity to show you are a content or industry expert.
- CURRENT: remain current on industry practices and new methods of networking such as the use of social media.

"The people you need to help your dream come true are everywhere, and within your reach." ~**Marcia Wieder**

I Have a Few Irons in the Fire

"Become a possibilitarian. No matter how dark things seem to be or actually are, raise your sights and see <u>possibilities</u> - always see them, for they are always there." ~**Norman Vincent Peale**

There comes a time as you continue trying to find work when you get frustrated answering the question, "So, how's it going?" I believe people who use this phraseology are asking about your personal well being and how you are emotionally. It is nice to have individuals care enough to ask how you are. You try to give an answer that is not three hours long, filled with bitterness and sarcasm, or reflects despair. People understand, especially in the early weeks after discharge that there is still a great deal going on in your head which you are trying to sort out.

Over time, as you continue to get this question, there is still the aspect of their concern for your emotional well being, but the intent of the question starts to shift focus to, "What opportunities do you have?" or "What are you working on? Any prospects?" This is a much harder question to feel good about answering if, for all intents and purposes, you have very little, if anything, in the way of real prospects. If you are in fact working hard and struggling to "land", then it can be extremely frustrating to have to report, "Nothing biting yet". You try to do so with a smile on your face and upbeat expression and inflection, but inside its killing you to have to respond, "Just the same old, same old".

Let me digress for a moment here. One thing many do not realize is that *looking for a job* is a *full time job*. True, you may not work at it

8-10 hours a day for seven days a week, but even if you are not directly engaged in an activity, it weighs on your mind 24/7. You are always wondering, thinking, plan "B-ing", and "what if-ing" (right?). But I have this sense people think we are waking up late, watching Regis and Oprah, having lunch, doing about 1-2 hours of "searching", having some mid day coffee, hanging with our "journey" buds at Starbucks, etc. I often heard my wife talking on the phone saying, "He is *very* busy. He's working *all the time* on finding his next career." My wife would hang up the phone and say, "This is unbelievable, people think you are just chilling and watching TV all day!" My guess is someone needed an errand done and thought why not ask the "laid off" guy, he isn't busy (sort of like asking Mikey to eat the string beans; "he eats anything!"). God bless my wife for understanding how difficult this is from a time factor as well as the emotional aspect.

Now, I am not saying some individuals are not waiting for divine intervention, or a knock on the door (with a job offer or a Lottery check). If you are one of the "passive searchers" (to put it gently) then you may want to rethink your strategy. First, you are probably aggravating your spouse (see Chapter 9). Second you are sending the wrong message to your kids (about giving up). Third, your lack of effort will be noticed by many and not reflect well in your networking circle regarding your (lack of) drive and perseverance. Finally, working hard at getting something will give you information that is crucial to developing a backup plan. Recall, it's not likely that you will land in the same place (job title, industry, compensation), from where you came. You may need to recognize that "this is not Kansas anymore Toto".

Table 17: Average Time to Land (2010)
- 3-6 months for a professional or management position (Employment News)
- 9-12 months for an executive position (Impact Hiring Solutions)
- 29.9 weeks for individuals age 55 or older (AARP)
- 21.4 weeks for individuals under age 55 (AARP)

- 25 weeks for individuals looking for annual salaries of $40,000-$75,000 (EZine article)
- 30 weeks for individuals looking for salaries of $100,000 or more (EZine article)
- Rule of thumb is one month per $10,000 of annual income sought (Forbes)
- Overall average for individuals seeking employment is 30.2 weeks (CNN Money)

Back to the question, *"How's it going?"* For weeks, okay months, I would answer that question with a dissertation related to every glimmer of an opportunity that came my way. I would give a play by play of each and every inquiry, interview, resume response, phone call, casual conversation, you name it, that may have the remotest chance of developing into an inkling of something to perhaps follow up. I wanted the questioner to know what a sought after asset I was. Although I had genuine opportunities, I also wanted to make myself feel good and paint the picture that I was doing fine and everything was under control. Over time, I realized two things; one, they really weren't asking for a short story of my "journey" (this was easy to tell after they glazed over about the 3rd minute into the soliloquy). Secondly, I may have been sending the wrong message; *"I've got a lot going on and thanks but I don't need your help"*. I thought OOOOHHHH! That's *exactly* what I need–their help. So I decided to begin using a very common phrase, which as you can see has become the title of this chapter, *"I have a few irons in the fire"*. This response became easier to say and much more pleasant for others to hear. I would also note, *"I'm always looking for leads and would appreciate any opportunities"* they may come across. I would keep them updated should any of these "irons" materialize into a career action. Now, if they ask the follow up question "that's great, any you can talk about?", then I figure they are sincerely interested (not just being courteous) and there may be one or two which they would find interesting. If not, I can always defer to share "at the appropriate time", thus leaving a door open to get back with them AND feeling a little less self demoralized by not saying…."same old, same old".

I am not sure that the experts would agree with my philosophy and you will have to determine if it works for you, but it did not hinder me, and probably kept me from losing a number of engaged associates (those tired of the long dissertations and therefore running to hide when they saw me coming!)

Let's discuss these "Irons in the Fire" or better stated, your options. As you spend the first few weeks really devising your plan and understanding what you want to do for the rest of your life (yes that is a bit scary) you will basically be prioritizing and selecting (and de-selecting) your available options. You will have to consider geography, relocation possibility, types of industries, employment vs. ownership, consulting vs. employment, working for a small or large organization, full time or part time, need for medical benefits, management or individual contributor, etc. You begin to focus on Plan A, what you really want to do. Soon, you may decide although you are not giving up on Plan A, you better have a Plan B and C. Ask yourself, what am I willing to do? What am I absolutely NOT willing to do? For example, I was senior leader in a billion dollar organization. My wife and I live in a beautiful area of Pennsylvania where we have been for 30 years. Our children own homes within eight minutes of our home. Grandchildren are hopefully in our future. I am not willing to leave this area.

In my most recent profession, healthcare, there were a number of executive positions available throughout the United States. None of which were within the one hour driving distance I determined was doable. This constrained my options significantly with respect to "landing" a senior executive position in healthcare, however, I did have other options as I had been in manufacturing for 13 years, owned a small business, consulted, and served on the board of directors of many non-profit organizations.

I took all this information, as well as what my needs were for compensation and formulated my plan (including preliminary thoughts on a contingency plan). This allowed me to evaluate opportunities as they arose. It also kept me from spending time chasing avenues that really would not meet any of my expectations (Plan C, D, or E!). This may fly in the face of what others say–look at everything that comes your way.

And to some degree I concur, but should you really fly to Detroit, if there is absolutely no way you would consider moving there? Some say, go for the experience of interviewing. I say, don't be disingenuous to the recruiter, the potential employer or yourself. If there is no way you are moving, it will become evident in the interview.

Try to be as open minded as you can with your planning. Would you be interested in buying a business, starting a business, or owning a franchise? There are tools out there to test your interest and preparedness for such a challenge.

If you believe you might be interested in owning a business, there are numerous national and international business brokerage firms. There are also companies which focus on particular regions and states. Table 18 offers a starting place to help you assess whether using a business broker is in your best interest.

Table 18: Websites for Buying a Business

- BizBrokerages.com
- Bizilla.com
- Bbnbrokers.com
- Globalbx.com
- Brokerservicesnetwork.com
- W3businessadvisors.com
- Americanbusinessbrokers.com
- Empirebb.com
- Brokersnetworkgroup.com
- Bizop.com
- Vrbrokerfranchises.com
- Bizbuysell.com
- Bizquest.com
- Buybusiness.com

Have you considered consulting, or coaching as an alternative career? Maybe you are entitled to a pension and can be covered by your spouses' medical and dental. If so, do you really need to work fulltime? What if you have been in the for-profit world your entire career? Maybe working or leading a local non-profit organization would be a fulfilling change? There is nothing more rewarding than working in a truly mission based company that addresses the health and human service needs of the community. I have three friends all of whom have been senior executives for most of their working career (in banking, healthcare and manufacturing). All three have taken leadership roles in local human services agencies, getting paid less than they were accustomed, but feeling absolutely great about what they are doing. Each has told me how they cannot wait to get to work and advance the mission of their respective institution. Granted, their circumstances are such that they can take the "comp" cut. Not everyone can do that. My point is, think about where you are in life, think what compensation and benefits you *must* have, and what options you absolutely will not consider. Then make a *list,* make a *plan.*

Your "irons" may surprise you. You may find yourself looking actively in a defined area or in a specific industry for a position with less stress and hours than you experienced previously. Or, you may consider starting or buying a business. Table 19 notes helpful websites as you evaluate your options.

Table 19: Career Opportunity Websites
- theladders.com
- careerexplorer.net
- myplan.com
- about.com
- careercast.net
- yahoo!hotjobs.com
- careerbuilder.com
- monster.com
- jobfox.com
- indeed.com
- simplyhired.com
- net-temps.com

At some point you may have to focus on 1-2 irons. For example, if you are considering acquiring a business, that will require a great deal of focus and time. If you have the possibility of doing some consulting, that could put a hold on pursuing other options. And, you may want to use this time to pursue a higher degree of education. The best scenario would be if you can evaluate one option without closing the door on another.

Keep in mind that there will be ups and downs. Sometimes more irons in the fire, sometimes just the fire. Don't become discouraged. I know, this is easier said than done, but the fact that you are getting opportunities, even if somewhat of a long shot, suggests you are trying, still in the game and not giving in. The key will be to know when to cut an option loose and when to focus on another more viable one. This will require evaluating the "end game" of each option (what will be the best that comes from this opportunity?), the risk associated with the time you spend pursuing (opportunity cost of passing on other prospects) and when the option has expired. Or as Kenny Rogers sings, "…Know when to hold them, know when to fold them, know when to walk away". I don't spend a lot of time listening to country music but this is pretty good advice!

It's hard to tell when to start the process of considering plan B or C. There will be a lot of personal factors that will drive that. A probable trigger will be your financial situation or your health benefits needs. In this day and age, many may need to consider implementing Plan B sooner. It is not that you are defeated. It is just that the new normalcy is here and you are doing what needs to be done to provide for your family and yourself. To do nothing, on principle, and jeopardize your family's health and well being is just not wise. Think about it. It's not only about you.

> **"Don't be discouraged, it is often the last key in the bunch that opens the lock."** ~**Author Unknown**

Is He Driving You Nuts Yet?

"Let the wife make the husband glad to come home, and let him make her sorry to see him leave". ~Martin Luther

I cannot help but think about the opening line of "A Tale of Two Cities" by Charles Dickens, *"It was the best of times, it was the worst of times"*. Actually this is probably better suited to the perception of the spouse as he, or she, goes through this process. It can truly become a test of love (or better stated; a test of strength!).

My wife is a saint, always has been, always will be. She is as understanding and supportive as you can hope for. At the beginning of this "journey" she was as upset as I was. Still, she has been one constant optimistic force continually saying, and believing, "This too shall pass". My wife has a deep and abiding faith in God, and confidence in me. What a gal.

I probably don't need to tell you how critical it is to have someone support and accept what you are going through. For those who were always working or preoccupied with work, even while at home, there is a feeling in the early weeks after your discharge that "it's good to have him/her home" and to enjoy some time together. Many individuals take some of the down time from the search to reconnect with their loved ones and maybe catch up on doing some things together which were set aside due to the hectic work schedule. It is unfortunate, but in the real world you were diligent (maybe too diligent) to prove your commitment and loyalty to the company and to secure your position (by the way, how did that work out for you?). So now you have more time with your loved one–maybe *much* more time–maybe TOO much time!

Why do I say that? Well, somewhere around the second month, I noticed a subtle shift in the questions my wife was being asked. The shift went from, "How is *HE* doing?" to, "How are *YOU* doing?" Being an industrial engineer by training I am adept at picking up such nuances, although quite frankly, it didn't take a rocket scientist to figure this one out. This transitional question as I call it, became the precursor for what people really wanted to ask… if I was driving my wife nuts. Finally, someone slipped and I actually heard the direct version, "Is he driving you nuts yet?" I thought OOOOHHHH…what's up with that?! And what am I doing to cause such a presumptive question?! I then asked my wife, "How many people ask you this?" She smiled–I hate when they just smile.

But of course, I couldn't leave it alone and asked *one of those questions*–you know, the kind of question that at the moment it comes out of your mouth, you wish you could immediately retract it! But, ignoring my better judgment, I pressed on asking my wife, "*Do they ever ask if YOU are driving ME nuts yet?!*" I know, I know–feel free to call me an idiot! I can hear you anyway! Well, after what seemed like an hour long silence (probably only a few seconds), I babbled something and tried to yank my foot from my mouth. The taste of sneaker remains.

For some of you, probably more of a generational thing, your spouse may be home during the day. A stay at home mom, or stay at home dad, or just working part-time to add some income to the household. This is probably the perfect scenario for potential disaster. Think about it, you are now spending more time in the house, even if you are diligently looking for work.

I think the problem is one of perception. Still in executive mode, you perceive that you have an inalienable right to make decisions in the house and to change things as you see fit. How wrong you are! You are a visitor, a temporary squatter, who, if there is a God, will be back out of the house within a few months. Your "observations" of how the household is run are best kept to yourself unless you have a death wish. You may have been the boss at work, or at least in control of your environment, but this is a different "hood" my friend!

My advice is to recognize and respect the "space" that your spouse has been adeptly managing in your absence. Imagine how you would feel if they called you at work during the day and told you what needs to be done and how to handle every situation. So, if you want to keep the peace at home, and make everyone's life a little less stressful (mainly yours), keep your mouth shut!

A better alternative is to understand that you may have some time to be helpful and to take on some tasks that can fill your down time and ease some of the stress around the home. Keep in mind that you may have been on the receiving end of having the household taken care of. It could be time to give back. This is up to you, but remember, your situation affects everyone and even if you believe it is "not your job" or "I was an executive, I don't do dishes", here's another news flash, you are unemployed and have time to do your fair share. Think about it.

Now some of you are in the situation where your spouse is working outside the house. (I phrase it this way since some believe that taking care of the home is not a job or "working" ....try it; then let me know if you still feel that way!). This scenario may buy you more time before the potential storm hits. There is less contact anxiety since you are not side by side all day, but there are still pitfalls to avoid. First, you may be bored at times, while your better half is at work. Don't take the liberty to call constantly and ask dumb questions or just to say "hello". That will seem cute in the beginning but will get tiresome over time. It's not that you are not loved or that the person does not understand your pain, it's just that they have a job to do. So, think twice before calling to ask, "*Where's the peanut butter?*" Or, "*What are we having for dinner?*" (*That one* is sure fire sleeping on the couch material!).

Stay focused on working your network, researching jobs, going to the outplacement center (if you have access), or taking some courses to learn new opportunities. The key to success here and avoiding another life altering event (divorce!) is to focus on the following: **Boundaries, Understanding, Courtesy, Kindness, Intuitiveness** and **Talking**, or simply, "BUCKIT". When things are getting a bit testy, just think, "BUCKIT"! Before you start or engage in any argument, stop and think, "BUCKIT". This acronym can be used as a mantra to keep the peace and facilitate coexistence during the "journey". When you see a storm rising just say over and over, *"BUCKIT, BUCKIT, BUCKIT"*!

Table 20 offers a sampling of websites that can assist you in understanding "conflict management", particularly in the home. Give these websites a glimpse, it may save you some grief!

Table 20: Conflict Management Websites
- focusonthefamily.com
- about.com
- ehow.com
- relationship-compatability-advice.com
- ask.com
- suite101.com
- powertochange.com

So, hopefully when your spouse is asked, *"Is he driving you nuts yet?"* She will say, *"You would think so, but we've worked on making sure that doesn't happen. When it looks like things are going sour, we just remember to BUCKIT"*!

For those of you who are accompanying someone on the "journey" please remember to be patient with your spouse. I cannot reiterate enough the emotional turmoil the "displaced" must try to overcome. Until they "land" they are feeling they may have let you and others down, they are floundering in ambiguity and are descending from a place of respect and perhaps authority to being one of those unemployed poor souls who got caught up in "whatever". The higher the position and the bigger the ego, the steeper the fall, the more patience you will need as it may take longer to land on their feet.

Remember to be a confidant and sounding board, and yes, even endure the venting. Hopefully that will subside over time and it may take your "intervention" to get them over a hurdle. Be open, honest and empathetic. Listen to what they need to say, but gently remind them it's time to move forward and you will remain by their side.

> *"The ultimate measure of a man is <u>not</u> where he stands in moments of comfort and convenience, but where he stands at times of challenge and controversy."* ~**Martin Luther King, Jr.**

Fuggedaboutit
Consulting Services, Inc

"Twenty years from now you will be more disappointed by the things you didn't do then by the ones you did. So throw off the bow lines. Sail away from the safe harbor. Catch the trade winds in your sails. Explore. <u>Dream</u>." ~Mark Twain

I was having dinner with my family one evening when my daughter asked how things were going and if I was OK. In true Italian-American Brooklynese I said, *"Fuggedaboutit, I'm doing fine!"* I told her someone asked me to give them a hand with a business problem. It was with this opportunity that I considered moving into the consulting world. And that's when it came to me... "Fuggedaboutit Consulting". *"You got a problem? Fuggedaboutit! Let me take care of it!"* (For those who have trouble with certain dialects, I am saying "forget about it"). By the way, that term "Fuggedaboutit" was made famous by the "mob shows", Goodfellas, Casino, Godfather, Sopranos etc, but where I grew up it was one of the first words you learned, *"Fuggedaboutit"* then *"mama" and "dada"*—in that order. And you need to abruptly wave your hand into the air at the same time you say it or you will immediately be recognized as a "wanna be Paisano".

Back to the point at hand–consulting. I wish I had a dollar for everyone who was laid off that wanted to own a restaurant, write a book (yeah, I know), and consult. I can speak as someone who has done all three and let me suggest that you think twice or three times before entering into the food business! Talk about hard work, long hours and stress. Just because you like to cook or eat, does not qualify you to be a restaurateur!

I suspect there have been an additional million new consultants over the past couple of years. When I ask those on the journey, "What do you have going on?" a significant percent say they are consulting or plan to consult, especially until they find a permanent landing spot. Some truly want to consult. They have paid their dues for years, have gained a great deal of knowledge and expertise which they believe can be shared with others, and be self-employed. Sounds like a utopian solution. For some it may be. The experts will tell you to stay viable as you search. One way to do that would be to consult. If you are fortunate enough to have a strong network, particularly a local one, you may have the opportunity to do some short term consulting or coaching, which I will talk about later.

Table 21: Benefits of Being a Consultant

- Most consultants earn approximately 30% - 50% more than their "employed" counterparts
- Consulting engagements are a potential means to "get your foot in the door" of an organization with which you may have interest in a "permanent" position
- There will be greater access to top levels of leadership of the client company and an opportunity to assess whether there is still interest on your part to be a "permanent" part of the organization
- More flexibility in your schedule during engagements
- Flexibility to choose assignments, determine your overall work time commitment and seek a quality of life balance
- Ability to build and expand the breadth and depth of your skills by exposure to diverse assignments
- Exposure to a variety of work environments, problem resolution and professional interactions which can be challenging, invigorating, and self-fulfilling

- Freedom from corporate or office politics and ongoing staffing related issues
- Investing in yourself as a "brand" to the extent that you determine
- Potential to develop a home-based operation including internet consulting
- You determine if you want to work 24/7 or be off the clock when the day is done
- Basically, *You* are the boss, owner, and decision maker for your company.

If you feel comfortable with the project scope and the location of the job, I would encourage you to consider taking on a consulting opportunity. As you look for the next great job or career, this can serve as a valuable resume builder. According to recent statistics, it takes an average of five to six months to find a new position. If you are a senior leader or a C-suite executive, the average is closer to 12-18 months. Based on that statistic, there is a high probability that you will have at least a six month gap (greater during difficult economic times) of inactivity on your resume. As the duration of inactivity increases you run the risk of raising a degree of concern about your "hire-ability", particularly if you are in an industry where technology, regulations, and best practices change rapidly.

I noticed as time passed, I was using the phrase, "I'm consulting" a lot more. It was true in a sense since I had done a two month engagement fairly soon after my release, but I think there was more to it than that. There was definitely a degree of comfort in telling others that I was "still in the game" and "there was a need for my abilities". You may experience this same emotional need to consider consulting as a short term band aid. You can not only do some good, but perhaps have an "inside shot" with the client should a position become available. What you must weigh is whether taking this short term engagement will distract you from your search and if there is an "opportunity cost" associated with the decision. What more permanent opportunities might you be passing up?

Accepting a consulting job, especially early in your search, can have another advantage; if you are confidently saying, "I can consult", and you are seriously considering being your own boss, this may be the ticket to test that interest. Unless you join a consulting firm as a contributing independent contractor, you will be operating your own business. At the outset, you may want to simply operate as a sole proprietor and claim the revenue on your personal taxes (I strongly recommend you discuss with your tax professional). You will also be responsible for your expenses and marketing your services. This will give you a taste of being your own boss and will offer insight into the world of consulting. Remember, it may be advantageous to take on some short term projects to keep active, visible, viable, and, to fill that "gap" on the resume. Table 21 notes the benefits of becoming a consultant.

Another alternative to consulting is "business coaching", commonly referred to as simply "coaching". This is a field gaining momentum; particularly since numerous talented leaders have been displaced in recent years. Coaching is defined as "the practice of providing support and advice to an individual or a group in order to help them recognize ways they can improve the effectiveness of their business. It can be accomplished in a number of ways, including one-on one interaction, group coaching sessions and seminars". As noted on one coaching website:

> *"Coaches work with clients to identify what is most important to them and align their thoughts, words and actions, accordingly."*
> *"Coaches work with clients to identify what they want personally and professionally, and to support them in achieving a life they really want and love."*
> *"Coaching offers a means for more balance, joy, intimacy, energy, financial abundance, focus and action in every area of life."*

Coaching is different than consulting. Consulting generally results in giving clients the answer, a plan to meet an objective. Coaching is focused on the clients arriving at their own answers through working with the coach as a partner, rather than a contractor (which is typical in hiring a consultant). Coaching is a long term, consistent, relationship. Consultants are in and out on episodic projects. It takes special characteristics to become an effective coach. They're similar in some part to becoming an effective consultant, but there are key differentiators, as shown in Table 22.

Table 22: Key Characteristics of a Coach vs. a Consultant

COACHES	CONSULTANTS
Focus on client's self-discovery and learning	Focus on task problem solving and giving direction
Guides the client through a journey by asking questions that the client answers	Guides the client through a problem solving process by answering questions which the client asks
Builds relationship with client that is long-term and focuses on the client's quality of life	Solves business problems on an episodic, intermittent basis and focus on the specific issue at hand
Works one on one on a relationship between client and coach that is on a personal basis	Works with organization or group of individuals on a purely business basis
Assists in identifying the client's dreams and fulfillment of professional and personal growth	Assists in identifying organizational needs and achieving results based on agreed upon expectations
Holds client accountable for agreed upon action plan	Does not have accountability upon completion of the engagement

There are a number of coaches out there. Many consulting businesses have added this service to their portfolio. There are also national and international companies that specialize in coaching. Table 23 notes a partial list of coaching company websites.

Table 23: Sample of Coaching Companies
- exe-coach.com
- vistage.com
- impactfactory.com
- successwithjack.com
- effectiveexecutiveleadership.com
- wabccoaches.com
- mariposaleadership.com
- powertransitions.com
- coachville.com
- abetterperspective.com
- richdadcoaching.com
- harmonycc.net
- robbinsmadanestraining.com
- sherpacoaching.com
- elearners.com
- brighttreecg.com

One final thought on coaching: don't get involved with coaching and interpersonal one on one relationships, or even team development, if you are just dabbling. If that is your intent, just *fuggedaboutit*, and move on to Plan B or C. However, if taken serious, coaching can be very rewarding, both serving as a coach as well as using a coach. The value of a coach is referenced in Table 24, while Table 25 offers the characteristics of a success coach.

Table 24: The Value of a Coach
Whether you become a coach or use a coach, coaching:
- Helps in clarifying personal vision and goals
- Provides objective support and a sounding board
- Focuses on developing momentum and moving things forward
- Helps in determining what matters and what needs to be focused on or delegated

- Assists in an objective look at what has been done and what has not been done
- Identifies effective behavior to achieve goals
- Expects accountability and rejects excuses to getting things done
- Evaluates and challenges productivity and outcomes to accomplish more
- Identifies fit of abilities with current role, responsibilities and goal expectations
- Identifies core values and principles and how they correspond with career expectations and goals

Table 25: Characteristics of a Successful Coach
- Authentic and Trustworthy
- Empathetic and Compassionate
- Patient and Dedicated
- Well-Rounded and Experienced
- Accessible and Committed
- Motivational and Inspiring
- Creative and Collaborative
- Organized and Focused
- Articulate and Communicator
- Positive Attitude and Supportive
- Approachable and Sense of Humor
- Poised and Professional

"We are kept from our goal not by obstacles but by a clear oath to a lesser goal." ~**Robert Brault**

If I Get My Real Estate License...Shoot Me!

"Energy and persistence conquer all things." ~ Benjamin Franklin

First, let me apologize up front for what I am about to say. I know there are extremely qualified and talented realtors, those who have spent a lifetime practicing their profession. I have always been especially impressed with those "lifers" who practice in the commercial market. One of my responsibilities at my former employer (getting easier to say without editorializing as time goes on...did you notice?), was handling the real estate properties which they owned. So I had a great deal of interaction with both residential and commercial realtors. As in any profession, there are those who are talented, those who are mediocre, and those who are absolutely horrible at what they do.

It is my theory that the marginal are basically those who had been "outplaced" from another career. They had no intention of ever functioning in the real estate world. After a change of life (for whatever reason) they heard a commercial on the radio or TV that said "YOU can enter the EXCITING and LUCRATIVE world of real estate", or, "come to our no cost introductory session and learn how, within just a couple of months, YOU can be a real estate professional!" Right there should be the "tell" (I watch a little World Tour Poker with my mother-in-law). *"PROFESSIONAL"*, in only 2 months!!! Geez, it takes 6 months to be a massage therapist. Sign me up for selling houses!

So now you take the required two classes (at least in my state), take a test and find a broker (who is the real professional—and it takes *years* to get to that level), who will "hang your shingle". Then go out in the market where there are millions of other "real estate professionals" all trying to sell the same 100 houses or move the same 100,000 square feet.

Personally, I think it becomes the last resort for many and thus my chapter title. The title came to me when a friend of mine, who had just crossed the Rubicon and signed up for the first course, said, "You can do this, André, why not sign up and we can attend together?" I graciously said, "Hmmm! Let me think about it". When we parted, I immediately called my wife and said, *"If I go for my real estate license...shoot me!"* My wife laughed with understanding since it took us 5 years and about 20 "professionals" to find our home. In the end, it was actually my wife who found it by driving around the neighborhood. (As a side note: our neighbor across the street is a *true professional* in the residential market. We wish we knew her during our search.)

If you are, or were, a realtor, or have a friend or family member that is, I am sure you are e-mailing me now with the 1000 reasons why this is truly a profession, the dedication and time needed to excel and be "best of class' is arduous. *Please, before you hit the "send" key, read the first paragraph of this chapter, again.*

What I'm trying to say is there may come a point where you are starting to feel some desperation. I know that time happened to me around 7-8 months and due to my criteria NOT to leave my area, my irons were cooling off. You get tempted to dive into what the marketers push your way (like being the next great realtor). Be wary of "jumping the shark[1]". Nothing is as easy as it seems. You may in fact have your real estate sales license and a broker to sponsor you...but you still have to SELL and CLOSE deals. You will truly be out there with those who have worked in your market for decades. And you may be jumping in at

---

1   **Jumping the shark** is an idiom used to describe the moment of downturn for a previously successful enterprise. The phrase is thought to have originated from a 1977 episode of "Happy Days" when the character, Fonzi, "jumped over a shark" while water skiing. The scene was widely criticized as a desperate attempt to revive the ratings.

a housing or commercial leasing downturn. Now you have committed time to learning, testing, finding a broker, etc. and you do not have dollar one for your effort. You have to list properties, show properties, and sell properties. Time, patience, perseverance and smiling (a lot of smiling) are the personal characteristics at which you must excel. You *must produce* since the agency cannot carry you forever. The broker may be your friend or family member, but never forget it is a business and I doubt they have a non-profit motive.

While you are preparing for your "new profession" you may be distracted from seeking or really prospecting for that opportunity which better suits you, your experience, and in some cases, can be the capstone on your career. The real estate illustration is really just a metaphor related to reacting to the fear and concern that will develop as the "journey" continues. This may be likened to buying a restaurant, becoming a "financial advisor" (don't get me started on that one!), or going into business with a family member (perish the thought).

All these venture or career changes are not quick fixes to the situation. You must think through them and research the pro's and con's. It appears too easy to jump into one of these low barrier to entry, short learning curve (or so the ads say!) fields that will bring you back to your previous financial state in the blink of an eye. You know the saying…"if it sounds too good to be true, it probably is" (or something like that).

If you are getting to that point where you are anxious enough to pull the trigger on something, I want to encourage you to talk to your spouse, family or a close friend. It is helpful to speak with someone you trust who can be objective (at least reasonably objective). For example, if you talk to your mom and dad from the Great Depression Era, you will probably jump at the first available potential source of income. That generation has a perspective on things that may be different from our generation and therefore less objective. I'm not saying they're wrong, but keep their frame of reference in mind. My mom called me every day (until she passed away—before I landed) to ask if I had a job yet. Those were the hardest calls emotionally–we will discuss in Chapter 12. Mom would say, *"Maybe you need to lower your sights, not be so picky, remember your roots.*" It is prudent to research what downside may exist with this quick fix option.

About mid-journey, I was approached by an extremely successful international coaching firm which has a distinguished reputation. I was aware of their approach to coaching and was intrigued by the opportunity to become part of the team. During the approval process to become a member of this organization (as an independent contractor), I attended existing group coaching sessions to observe. I talked to those being coached and asked a great deal of questions. It all sounded great. It positively fit with my skill set, my passion to work with leaders (upcoming and seasoned) and being in control of my time. It could be lucrative assuming you were coaching 2-3 groups. At 4 groups, very lucrative.... matching my senior executive salary without leaving the area!

Is there a downside? In my geographical area, the answer is yes. Do your due diligence. In the case of the executive coaching it was the risk of not being able to pull enough groups (clients) together. If you don't have a large network, this could prove difficult. The "payout" doesn't come until you hit critical mass. And, in the area I would be serving there are already 5 established coaches, a couple who are struggling. It typically takes 4-5 months to pull your *first* group together. During that time, little, or even no income is coming your way. On top of that, by asking the right questions, I learned that 40-50% of "new coaches" *never* get that first group together. And, that the average number of groups per coach is around 2 (after many years at it). Those that have 3 or 4 groups (making the big bucks) are rare, very rare. Five groups put you in the Hall of Fame!

OK, now I know the upside and the downside and can make an informed (not emotional) decision. I did, and decided to pursue the (very thorough) approval process. I should add that this organization did not in any way misrepresent itself and responded to my various questions. While comprehensively researching both sides of this opportunity, I continued to pursue other opportunities. This gave me a couple of months to vet this opportunity against others before making a final decision. The outcome of my decision can be found in Chapter 16.

The takeaway from this chapter is to remain open minded, expand the scope of your search, be prudent, BUT do not get caught up in the "hype", don't be blinded or afraid to the point that you overlook doing your due diligence. Remember that vetting your thoughts with those you trust and who will challenge you in a constructive manner, will be extremely beneficial. You will know when you have hit that time when it is necessary to do something, *anything*, in order to eat and take care of your family. Many may come to that end game sooner than anticipated, particularly in these difficult economic times. In that case, "you have to do what you have to do". It actually takes someone with tremendous character to step up in that situation. All I urge is that you be prudent and informed.

"When you come to the end of your rope, tie a knot in it and hang on." ~**Franklin D. Roosevelt**

Things Will Work Out...
Mom Said So!

"The only limit to our realization of tomorrow will be our doubts of today. Let us move forward with strong and active faith." ~Franklin D. Roosevelt

Throughout the "journey" there will be good days, bad days and REALLY bad days. There may even be times when you want to just give in and say Freak it! What happens is what I call "late wakeup creep" (think of repeatedly hitting the snooze button). At the outset you are still programmed to awaken the same time you did for years, follow the "bathroom" routine, dress, get your coffee and out the door. Maybe, in a few weeks, you think, "just five more minutes" when you awaken by internal alarm. Then five minutes becomes 10 minutes, 10 becomes 20…30, and then one hour–and the next thing you know you're watching Fox and Friends or the Today Show (depending on your political leaning) and even Regis and Kelly are becoming a morning staple.

Be wary of "creep" and be mindful of how you are drifting emotionally. This is where having a great support system is imperative. You may not detect the small incremental changes that you are experiencing… wake up creep, easily diverted to do other things that are not progressing your search, being generally in a more somber mode, using negative imagery like "this will never end", or "I will be sitting here doing nothing for another 6 months", or starting to play the victim card again.

You need to surround yourself with people who are positive, encouraging and believe in you. But it's more than just mom saying, "*Things will work out*". Yes these compassionate words help and may get you through a rough day, but in reality this is a lot of work, perseverance, doggedness, and grinding. You will need to be able to project enthusiasm, positivity, and composure, even in the face of adversity, frustration and rejection. It's about never giving in.

There will be days where you need to back off, reflect, catch your breath and reevaluate your plan. I found it helpful to actually build that "reflection" time into my schedule. That always worked for me as an administrator. It always amazed me how little some other administrators got accomplished or struggled to meet deadlines because they allowed every minute of the day to be taken by meetings. They never blocked out what I would call "desk time" to take stock of where they were in achieving goals. They would simply think that they will "find time" throughout the week. I recall one senior leader who eloquently stated "what we need in our jobs is time to think!"

Plan for "desk time" to refresh your thinking and take stock of where you are and where you need to go. The planning process is as important, if not more so, then the actual plan. The plan will change... never met a plan that didn't. It's the process that is critical. Don't let reflective time be a happenstance....build it in.

It is always a boost to hear from others that "things will be alright", we all need that. My Rock of Gibraltar has been my wife and children. Their confidence in my ability and their concern for my well being is a constant reminder that things will turn out fine. But, positive thinking, although a powerful tool, does not pay the bills. So, let the encouragement keep you charged up and focused. But stay out there and work hard to find a landing.

When mom called me, every day, and I mean *every* day...to see how I was doing, she would assure me all will be well (that's what mom's and dad's do). It had an immediate calming effect (which is interesting because if you knew my mom, "calming" wouldn't be the first word that came to mind!). But there was more to the interaction for me. I felt she and my wife, among others, were really telling me how confident they were that I would prevail, that I have much to offer. I felt I could not let them down and have them continuously concerned about my future. So, instead of leaving it *all* to faith, draw from the strength of those around you and get on track. Maybe you don't need to wake up at the break of dawn each day, but be consistent, develop a routine, get (or stay) organized and focused.

Pay attention to what you are feeling emotionally and physically. Contact a health care professional if you are sensing some change or if your spouse is noticing a difference in your mood or demeanor. It is not a failure to seek outside counsel, be it your family doctor, your clergy, or even a therapist. This is a traumatic event and over time, if the end game is still not clear and you are worrying more and sleeping less, then you may want to make that appointment.

Table 26 notes the tell tale signs of stress and its effects on your body, thoughts, feelings, and behavior. It is not intended to replace your healthcare professional, but may give you cause to make that call.

Table 26: Stress Symptoms: Effects...[2]

...on Your Body	...on Your Thoughts and Feelings	...on Your Behavior
Headache	Anxiety	Overeating
Back pain	Restlessness	Undereating
Chest pain	Worrying	Angry outbursts
Heart disease	Irritability	Drug or alcohol abuse
Heart palpitations	Depression	Increased smoking
High blood pressure	Anger	Social withdrawal
Decreased immunity	Feeling insecure	Crying spells
Stomach upset & Sleep problems	Lack of focus, Burnout, and Forgetfulness	Relationship conflicts

2   Source: Mayo Clinic website, www.mayoclinic.com

All of us tough guys want to gut it out. Ok, I get it. But if things start slipping away, you could wind up in a bad place. This is a good time to see your doctor, get that annual physical you've been putting off and take this opportunity to tell him/her what you are going through and feeling.

One of the keys in my mind to getting through this is to exercise and eat healthy. Unfortunately I didn't exactly practice what I preach, and that was a lost opportunity. Set aside time, maybe early morning, or after dinner, to exercise. Also, it is too easy to develop nightmarish eating habits as you get out of your routine and have additional access to the kitchen. For those who were less at the desk and more active throughout the day, this could provide a real challenge. Even if you are at home working on the computer, writing, and calling contacts, it becomes too easy to find that snack and drink that caffeine as your number of "breaks" begin multiplying!

I am not a nutrition expert and certainly not ready for the cover of "Modern Health", but I did have to sit down every so often and have a talk with myself about eating junk and forgetting to exercise. Try to take some of this time to change bad habits into positive lifestyle changes. If you can accomplish this before you "land" you will be that much further ahead of the game. Although it is discrimination at its worst, I believe that a (perceived) healthy candidate will have an edge over those who appear to be neglecting themselves. You may never hear that from the interviewer but it's reality check time.

The moral of this chapter is: "Yes, mom says it will be alright, and it probably will, but NOT if you simply *wish* it to happen and don't work at it". Stay mentally and physically healthy and work at finding that new opportunity. Of course, if your mom (or dad) is Owner/CEO of a multi-billion dollar company, you could have skipped this chapter. Sorry, should have said that in the first paragraph.

> *"If you can't sleep, then get up and do something*
> *instead of lying there worrying. It's the worry that*
> *gets you, not the lack of sleep."* ~**Dale Carnegie**

Maybe it's Time for the American Dream

"Whatever course you decide upon, there is always someone to tell you that you are wrong. There are always difficulties arising which tempt you to believe that your critics are right. To map out a course of action and follow it to an end requires....courage."
~Ralph Waldo Emerson

Have you ever thought to yourself..."if I only had a boss like me", or "I would do that differently", or "I can't believe they pay him (or her) to run this place, I could do a better job". Have you ever contemplated The American Dream...owning your own business? To some individuals this would be exciting. To others it may suggest a level of risk they are just not comfortable with. Small business and entrepreneurial spirit is a critical aspect of our economy and what we built our great country on. Immigrants came to America for many reasons, but certainly one was the opportunity to create a business and work for themselves. Table 27 illustrates the importance and impact of small businesses in our economy.

Table 27: Small Business Statistics[3]
The estimated 29.6 million small businesses in the United States:
- Employ just over half of the country's private sector workforce
- Hire 40% of high tech workers, such as scientists, engineers and computer workers
- Include 52% home-based businesses and 2% franchises
- Represent 97.3% of all the exporters of goods
- Represent 99.7% of all employer firms
- Generate a majority of the innovations that come from United States companies

Small Business Survival Rates: (Small Business Openings and Closings in 2008)
- There were 627,200 new businesses, 595,600 business closures and 43,546 bankruptcies
- Seven out of 10 new employer firms survive at least two years, and about half survive five years

Note: The office of Advocacy defines a small business for research purposes as an independent business having fewer than 500 employees.

"Work for yourself", that is an interesting idea. Having been a small business owner I can tell you that working for yourself sounds jazzy and euphoric. But it requires a great deal of work, diverse skill sets, perseverance, organization and checking your ego at the door (in some cases you are also doing the janitorial services!). If you do not have all the tools necessary to successfully conceive, plan and implement a new business, you need to acknowledge that and find resources to help. There are a plethora of them out there, including coaches, as discussed earlier. Table 28 summarizes a sampling of resources.

---

3   Source: U.S. Small Business Administration and U.S. Department of Commerce

Table 28: New Business Resource List:

allbusiness.com	welcomebbb.org, bizjournals.com
askjim.com	bizratios.com
askthelawyers.com	bizstats.com
ebay.com	bplans.com
entrepreneur.com	businessownersideacafe.com
export-u.com	franchiseregistry.com
asttrac.org	frannet.com
inc.com	gosmallbiz.com
jumpup.intuit.com	morebusiness.com
microsoft.com	quickmba.com
sbdcnet.org	score.org
smallbusiness3.com	thomas.net
smallbusinessdnb.com	welcomebusiness.com
restaurant.org	finance.yahoo.com
isquare.com	

Research, research, research are the three keys (followed of course by location, location, location which is more commonly referenced). Going into a new venture can be very risky, not only for you but your entire family. There are horror stories out there where people have invested their life savings into a business and were not qualified to run it and even worse, not realizing when to exit.

This still can be one of the most fulfilling aspects of your working life; building something on your own, watching it grow, reaping the benefits (assuming your success) and then (perhaps) watching your children take on the legacy when it is time for you to slow down; if you bring the entire family into the company (which has its pros and cons, as noted in Table 29), the endeavor can be even more rewarding.

Table 29: Pro's and Con's of a Family Owned Business
PRO's
- Higher degree of freedom, independence and control.
- A feeling of pride, prestige and family honor.
- Less bureaucratic (unless working with the government).

- There is a natural trust factor.
- Shared set of values.
- Loyalty due to family member's common goals.
- Built-in support system.
- A rich history that bonds the members.

CON's
- Conflicts with relatives can create issues.
- Unclear roles and responsibility due to avoidance of conflict.
- Communications issues between members created by non-business situations impacting workplace.
- Succession planning is often unplanned or based on emotion.
- Senior generation preventing younger generation from growing and leading.
- Family members who are passive investors vs. active participants.
- Interest in some members to use business to "bury" personal expenses.
- Difficulty counseling or disciplining family members.
- Placing unskilled members in roles they "want" rather than what they are suited for.
- Agreement on exit strategy, including dissolution, becomes personal and emotional rather than business focused.

My wife and I owned a fine art gallery. With my business background and network and her passion and marketing and artistic acumen, we decided to go for it. She would be the primary owner and run the day to day aspects of the business. I would provide financial oversight and coach and consult as she requested. We worked side by side for years. Sure it gets testy once in awhile (of course MY fault, not hers…just ask her!), but we worked as a partnership and had been successful on many levels, but with a great deal of work and many days and sleepless nights of stress.

This is probably not for everyone and if you were to ask any small business owner, it is the hardest job they ever had. The hours are non-stop, there is always something to do or plan, and the sweat equity is real (you actually sweat). In our case we watched our business flourish from a casual conversation we had three years prior to opening the business. This gave us a taste of the independence that can come from owning a business and being the key decision maker. You can claim all the credit when things are going great! But, you also have no one to blame if things are not going well. You can make strategic decisions and take action much quicker than by a committee process and 10 levels of decision makers than you were probably used to. The risk is there, but the reward and the personal satisfaction of having tried is hard to explain unless you have experienced it. Not for everyone, but definitely for some. And maybe you are one of those who will embrace the opportunity and begin a new journey.

While writing this book, the unemployment rate climbed past 10%, and the economy tightened. Combined this with more young people coming into the labor force, and older adults working longer, and it appears the available job situation will continue to be tentative. Even if by the time you read this book the unemployment rate is cut in half (which is very unlikely) the competition for jobs in the future will continue to grow on a global basis. You are not just competing with the local talent, but a worldwide talent pool, with some participants willing to work for significantly less income than our American lifestyle is accustomed (you may want to read "*The World is Flat*" by Thomas L. Friedman). Outsourcing by U.S. owned companies has become a way of business survival (ask the tech support guy from Bangor next time your computer goes on the fritz!).

All that being said, small business ownership could be the best avenue to take. There are a number of ways to enter the small business world:

- Start a business
- Buy an existing business
- Acquire a franchise

Each has benefits and risks. You should consult with your accountant and other advisors as you consider the options. A summary of aspects to consider when evaluating a business start-up or buying an existing business appears in Table 30.

Table 30: Buying vs. Starting a Business
Advantages of buying an established business:

- Known actual performance vs. projected pro-forma.
- Immediate cash flow.
- Brand awareness and equity.
- Product or service is a proven concept.
- Employees in place.
- Established customers.
- Established supplies.
- Existing inventory.
- Owner may assist with financing.
- Owner may assist with training.
- Process and policies in place.
- Licenses, permits and legal aspects in order.
- Risk profile is known.
- Information technology may be in place.
- Lower failure rate associated with proven businesses vs. high failure rate of start-ups.

Considerations of starting your own business:

- Developing an idea for a new business can be extremely rewarding and self-gratifying.
- The cost of acquiring an established business, including the premium for goodwill, can be greater than start up costs.
- If the acquisition is not structured as an asset purchase, contingent liabilities may be incurred with the purchase.

If you are considering the purchase of an existing business there are a number of things to evaluate. First, take some time to review the sample checklist included in the Appendix entitled, "Business Acquisition

Due-Diligence Checklist". A complete, more extensive checklist can be obtained at www.rennaconsulting.net.

Second, you should talk to a business acquisition specialist and your trusted advisors. There are business brokers that typically represent the seller but would have access to a portfolio of available businesses. This is a resource you can consider for access to the market. Recognize they are truly working for the seller. That said, there are many business brokers who are eager to assist you. A short list appears in Table 31.

Table 31: Business Brokers

bizbuysell.com	vrbusinessbrokers.com
marketfish.com	fbb.com
businessbrokers.net	bizbrokersinc.com
tworld.com	business.com
bizquest.com	fbba.com
worldwidebusinessbrokers.com	bizbrokers.com
amerivestbusiness.com	bacqs.com
lisitenassociates.com	fcbb.com
inforret.com	liasonbrokeragepartners.com
woodbridgegrp.com	thehortongroup.com

Franchising may be another avenue to consider. Franchises do come with "strings attached" and must be reviewed in great detail and with outside counsel. There is always a screening and approval process by the Franchisor which will vary by company. The financial fees will also differ although there is a basic methodology and range. The FFD document will be key to understanding the terms and conditions. REVIEW this in detail. I strongly urge you to have legal counsel review the document. Know what you are committing too. There will be restrictions and covenants that you will be bound by (as in any agreement). It is also key to understand what the franchisor does for the franchisee. Some are more active and engaged then others. The level of autonomy also varies. So if you have no interest in operating within certain constraints and boundaries, this may not be for you. If you are convinced that you want to operate your own business but like the idea of having resources available that are also invested in your success (most, if not all franchises take a percent of gross revenue and are therefore very motivated to have you succeed) this could be the ticket. Table 32 (Benefits of a Franchise) can be used to stimulate your thinking as to whether this is an option for you.

Table 32: Benefits of a Franchise
- Established trade name, logo, and marks
- Known and proven product or service, with established reputation
- Established business strategy and marketing plan with support from franchisor
- Ongoing support with operations, including existing policy and procedure manuals
- Assistance in location selection with market research and expertise of franchisor
- Training is provided at start-up and available on an ongoing basis as needed
- A start-up "tool kit" is available from franchisor
- Access to established suppliers and technical resources
- Selling the business may be facilitated by the franchisor

Keep in mind there are also franchise brokers out there who can help you through the process of deciding what type of franchise may suit your expectations as well as give you a sense of whether you would qualify financially. They are paid by the franchisor–remember that. A short list of franchise specialists is offered in table 33.

Table 33: Franchise Specialists

fransource.com	ifranchisegroup.com
forex.com	evancharmichael.com
sellfranchise.com	myfranchisepath.com
franchiseallianceinc.com	bizology.com

franchiseba.com	franchisebrokerguide.com
frannet.com	franchisebrokersassociation.com
franchiseattorney.com	bizbuysell.com
nextbigfranchise.com	franchisedirect.com
bestfranchiseinformation.com	franchisesolutions.com
franchisefinders.com	businessbrokerdirectory.com

There are also many resources at your disposal which are seller/buyer neutral. Many are government funded (SBA-Small Business Association, and SCORE) and at no cost to you. Others may have related fees, particularly if they involve seminars and educational materials. Your local Chamber of Commerce may also be helpful. Surf the web and you will find many more, including small business development resources at local colleges and universities. It's all about your risk and reward profile, your level of confidence in your business skills, your specific talents (e.g. electrician, chef, accountant, etc) and the financial and emotional state of you and your family. If this is something you have always dreamed about doing, and you have taken the time to genuinely research and plan, this may be your "landing" site.

"I know the price of success: Dedication, hard work
and an unremitting devotion to the things you
want to see happen." ~Frank Lloyd Wright

I Can Always Drive a Limo

"The courage of life is often a less dramatic spectacle than the courage of a final moment, but it is no less a magnificent mixture of triumph and tragedy. A man does what he must, in spite of personal consequences, in spite of obstacles, and dangers and pressures–and that is the basis of all morality." ~John F. Kennedy

It's one thing to offend realtors, but now I am probably going to offend limo drivers too. I know it's not fair to stereotype, but the limo guys I knew in Brooklyn were not the type of guys you wanted to take a shot at (no pun intended). So, if you are an "ex" or current limo driver, *Please* skip to Chapter 15!

The idea for this chapter came at dinner one evening with a friend who was experiencing the same concerns and frustrations that most of us feel as the search continued. We were just finishing our salad when he blurted out, "Well, I can always drive a limo!" He is also of Italian American decent, grew up in New York and living in Pennsylvania. After a brief chuckle, I thought to myself…hmmm, I'm 6' 1", have a black trench coat, can talk like the limo drivers in the movies, I like people, I like to drive…maybe this was right in front of me and I have been a bit "stunad" (as we limo guys say….or stupid for you non Italian Americans). I actually started to put this in my Plan E category. Unfortunately I think my friend had moved this up to his Plan B status and was dangerously flirting with it as Plan A.

In Chapter 11 we discussed not taking a drastic step too early and "giving in". It was also noted that there may come a time when decision making is at a critical point. It is at that time that you are probably weighing the need to produce income and obtain health benefits versus a job that is not a reflection of your experience, education, level of abilities, or previous compensation. If you are not on severance, ending your severance, done with unemployment compensation (or it just is not sufficient to meet your basic financial needs), then you may be more pressed to take something, anything that comes along. Again, be wary, but you will need to do what has to be done.

The idea of "I can always drive a limo" is more a metaphor for the hope that there is "*something* "out there. Maybe it has to be a "place holder" job until something breaks in your industry or area of expertise. I practiced every day saying "*Welcome to Costco, can I see your member-ship card?*" (Hey, you just never know). If you become faced with the difficult task of having to make a decision to "take something", don't consider this the end of the line, but a necessary crossroad in the overall plan. Or as Yogi Berra would say, "*When you come to a fork in the road… take it*". Difficult times call for difficult decisions, but it does not have to be considered the twilight of your career, unless you're ready for that phase of your life. Keep researching and making those contacts. If you have been following your plan and been proactive, you are already wired on how to do this. The messaging will have to change, reflecting that you have a temporary position, or job, but that you are still diligent in looking for an opportunity that positions you for the future.

If you really are not ready to complete the rest of your working life behind the wheel of a limo, or a checkout counter at Wal-Mart, or selling cars (we haven't even talked about that one!), then do not go into the job with this fatalistic attitude. There comes a time in everyone's life where they need to make sacrifices. This could be the short term sacrifice until you get that great landing.

Some may say this is a disingenuous way to be…accepting a job but continue looking. There may be circumstances where this is true. If you are hired by a firm that has passed on a number of other candidates and employed you with the expectation that you are there to stay, then you may feel you have a moral or ethical obligation to stop looking. However, all employers are just that...employers (remember the day you were told about your legacy...see Chapter 1 if you forgot already). I am not suggesting that you become a corporate whore, but this is about survival, yours and that of your family. Corporate America has changed the rules of the game. You need to act in your best interest. I would refrain from outright lying and saying "I am here to stay until death do us part". You will have to find the balance on this issue that works for you. I have told potential employers, "If the opportunity remains challenging, and we are meeting both our expectations and there are no significant life altering changes in my life, I am planning to stay on board".

Your ego will be a factor, especially for those who have been in leadership positions for a while. You may need to check it at the door for awhile. Perhaps you can find a part time job, some short term consulting, or interim leadership or project management position. Those opportunities may be more satisfying to you, if they are available. But the short term may bring you back to the "old days", when you started out, before you became "big time". Remember what Yogi Berra said, *"You give 100% in the first half of a game, and if that isn't enough, in the second half you give what's left"*. The "less than perfect" position may actually energize you. You may go into it with the attitude, "I'm just buying some time", but you may be surprised. Recall those three friends of mine that took positions in non-profit organizations. They are still going strong and have found a purpose larger than they anticipated. They remain very content in their roles and have been re-energized about their contribution to the community. Yes, they bring home less money, and no, the stress level is not totally gone, but the intrinsic value of what they do for the community has greatly overshadowed the other factors. You may be in the stage of life where this is truly the capstone of your career.

As time goes on and you really consider taking that Plan C job, your bitterness level will start to rise again, unless of course you have seen the light and made total peace with what has happened. Assuming you *really* haven't, don't be surprised that those "feelings" come back a little stronger as you face the reality that you may be starting all over again, or you may be forced to take on a job that your ego is struggling with.

Again, you are not alone in your feelings. I can only hope these feelings pass over time as they are very destructive. I imagine it is different for each person, but I have not encountered anyone yet who has simply come to peace with what occurred; unless they land in a more lucrative position or have truly found their "calling" and could not be happier.

Your friends and family as well as the career counselors will encourage you to take this chance to be what you have always dreamed to be. I say, sure, if it was just that simple; if it was only me I had to worry about; if I was 10 years older and ready to retire, or twenty years younger. Cop out, maybe, but when I have spoken to those who have landed, who seem content with where they landed, they don't seem upset that they blew another chance to "live the dream". I believe they are thankful for the stability and chance to be viable again. They may have learned something along the journey which may help them when they are truly prepared to wind down.

I am sure some individuals "land on fantasy island" and are thankful for the opportunity it gave them to "finish the dream". Most however find comparable jobs and settle back into the usual routine. Others, will drive limo's either for a while, or decide…Fuggedaboutit, this isn't so bad!

> **"I long to accomplish a great and noble task, but
> it is my chief duty to accomplish small tasks as if
> they were great and noble." ~Helen Keller**

Retirement? Pension? Hmmm...

"The road to happiness lies in two simple principles; find what interests you and that you can do well, and put your whole soul into it- every bit of energy and ambition and natural ability you have." ~ John D. Rockefeller III

Time passes. Maybe it's been 10-12 months since you began your journey. Hopefully you have been fortunate enough to evaluate different alternatives and find your next career. If not, perhaps you are keeping the faith and still persevering. If you have "landed" I hope you have completed your journey on a positive note and have found solace and content in your new endeavor. Throughout the journey you have no doubt gone through a myriad of emotions, starting at disbelief, progressing rapidly to anger, and then vacillating between excitement to despair (and everything in between).

You have had good days, bad days and horrible days. The emotional roller coaster demands every ounce of courage and optimism which you can muster. An event such as this is a test of a person's character. Throughout the journey, hopefully, you learned something about yourself and what is truly important to you; maybe you rediscovered friends and family, volunteered in your community, slowed your pace and enhanced your quality of life. You may have discovered a "new normalcy", a new way of life. And you know what? Maybe it's not that bad. All things considered, you not only survived but have found a joyful lifestyle and are poised to move on.

This scenario will not apply to all of the "journey takers". Not everyone lands where they expected or hoped to at the outset. If you are at a stage in life where you need to work; there is college tuition to pay, a new mortgage, sick parents to care for, or you are just not ready to retire (too young to join the shuffleboard league or for senior discounts at the movie theater and local diner), then keep your options open and continue the search.

There are some who may have had all the intentions in the world to land that next executive job, or open that business, or just get back into the 9-9 club (used to be 9-5 but let's face it, who works only 8 hours a day anymore?!). Over time, reality sets in. A simple realization there is more to life than the corporate politics and gamesmanship. The idea of retiring, or at least semi retiring, starts to become a consideration; understandably not for everyone, but there is certainly a segment of the displaced for who this may become a reasonable "landing". If you have a company pension, you may want to consider beginning the payments as soon as possible, though I recommend you seek the advice of a financial professional first. If your spouse has a job and access to health insurance, this may create the opportunity to rethink your situation.

The group that is mostly affected by this issue would be those who have been let go and are 55-65 years of age. The profile is probably something like this: 55 years old, empty nester, worked for their employer 20 plus years, have either risen to a leadership position or a key role as an individual contributor (top mechanic, senior salesperson, accounting manager, etc) and had planned to retire from the company.

These individuals are really in a tough spot. Not that others have it so sweet, but they are part of the sandwich generation. They may have elderly parents who need their support, and children who, if not at home or in college, are just beginning their careers or families who also need their support. To burden these individuals with the need to "find work" creates an additional level of stress. This is the group that will spend the most time laboring over whether they should grind it out, take a risk (new business) or cut back (semi-retire).

As I weighed my options, even earlier in my journey, there were a few interactions that really hit home. They came from a number of diverse and unsuspected sources. I grew up in a blue collar, strong work ethic, bread winner mentality. My folks were the classic WWII generation. Dad worked all day in the city (THE city–New York City). He was a strap hanger (no he didn't make straps; he rode the subway from Brooklyn to Manhattan, everyday–standing up, holding on to the "strap"). Mom was a stay at home mother and when we were tight on money, she worked part-time sewing in a factory near our home. Dad also did part-time jobs such as house painting and ushering in a movie theatre. So, my family always worked and didn't sit back on our laurels. So, imagine my surprise when my mother said to me, "*Why don't you just retire? You have a pension coming, you have worked so hard for years. Maybe it's time to slow down*". I am still shocked by this. I said, "*Mom, I'm only 55 and even though I can take an early pension, what would I do with myself?*" Her response still rings in my ear, "*Enjoy your life and your children and live longer*".

One day my adult daughter said to me, "*You know dad, we love having you around and spending more time with us*". I was again stunned as I am very close to my children, only 8 minutes away by car to each of them, and we do a great deal together (still try and get family trips in every couple of years although the destinations have become more expensive!). So when she said that, I was surprised and probably gave her the Vinny Barbarino response, "Huh?" She picked this up and said, "*I know you spend a lot of time <u>with</u> us, but you always seemed to be thinking of work, worrying about the job, preparing for your next project, or just preoccupied*". (Sound familiar?!)

Then my adult son suggested, "*Why don't you do something part time or invest in your own business and let someone else run it. Why would you want to go back to 12 hour days, the crap you put up with at your last employer, and for what...to be 'dumped'?. You paid your dues. It's time to chill*".

I have an Indian friend, Minu, for whom I have a great deal of respect. I've known Minu for almost 30 years and he's almost 20 years my senior. "Min", as I refer to him, has resided in the U.S. since completing college and has been a successful food product developer. Min has been retired for the past 12 years. He called me one day and we talked about my situation. Having worked together for years, he knew the level of intensity I displayed toward meeting expectations. He knew how driven I was and how I always wanted to contribute. Min reminded me there are other ways to contribute without putting in 12 hour days. He told me to go "stand on my head" (must be a yoga thing) and the inspiration will flow.

Maybe it was time to step back, get some balance and find additional means to fulfill my life. There were others too who echoed these feelings. It definitely gave me pause for thought. But I continued to work hard on my "landing". As time moved on and even though opportunities came my way, I continued to give some thought to the idea of "retiring", or maybe "semi-retirement". Having determined that I was not leaving the area (to stay close to my children and future grandchildren), I became very selective on considering any options. As time passed and the reality of my situation, particularly as it related to my commitment to staying put, the idea of not working at the level I had for so many years seemed like an alternative that maybe needed to be explored.

The transition from, "No way, I have too much work to do", started to seem less important as the months passed. In my situation, I didn't exactly retire, as I discuss in Chapter 16.

Don't look at this as an ending, but as a beginning. Consider the information in this book; use all of it or some of it. Refer back to the chapters as needed as a resource guide, or reread a chapter or two to remind yourself that you are not alone and that there is light at the end of the tunnel, if you persevere. Try to look at your journey as a step toward self-actualization and recognition. *There* IS *more out there,* all you have to do is look, then reach for it.

> *"Nobody can really guarantee the future. The best*
> *we can do is size up the chances, calculate the risks*
> *involved, estimate our ability to deal with them and*
> *make our plans with confidence."* ~Henry Ford II

Cleared For Landing

"If only the people who worry about their liabilities would think about the riches they do possess, they would stop worrying. Would you sell both your eyes for a million dollars... or your two legs...or your hands...or your hearing? Add up what you do have, and you'll find that you won't sell them for all the gold in the world. The best things in life are yours, if you can appreciate yourself." ~**Dale Carnegie**

As I write this final chapter I realize it has been almost exactly one year since I first sat down to plan *"You'll Land on Your Feet."* During that time I had to deal with the unfortunate and sudden passing of my mother. My mother, in addition to my wife and children, was a significant influence in my attempt to deal with this "journey". She reinforced, *"this too shall pass"* and *"you have never given up, you've always been able to adapt and succeed in all you've done, so stop whining and take care of business"*. Italian mothers have a way of putting things in such a "loving" fashion! However, she would also remind me to *"find the good even in what appears to be a bad situation"*. As hard as it was to lose my mother, her passing helped me regain perspective, a perspective that perhaps I was losing.

The "good" that came from this particular timing was that it snapped me back into the reality about what is most important in life; we are only here for a short period of time and we need to realize how precious that time is and make good use of it. We can choose to allow diversity to eat us up, or we can accept that bad things happen to good people. We can wallow on the "dark side" (remember "Star Wars"?), or we can focus on the blessings all around us. We can look at what happened as the end of our career (if you are close to retirement age), or we can look at it as an opportunity to embrace a new career path or capstone.

The life lessons my parents taught me are priceless. They continue to parent "from above", where no doubt, my mother is trying to teach the angels and saints a thing or two! (I can see them rolling their eyes from all the way down here!).

So the message I hope you receive from reading *You'll Land on Your Feet*; is to get your priorities straight, to adapt, and to never give up or give in. When it feels like your world has been turned upside down, when you've hit rock bottom, when you've had enough, consider that to be a time to take stock of who you are, what you really want in life, who and what is important to you, and how you can adapt to regain balance in your life.

As I am typing on my laptop, I notice a piece of paper which I previously taped below the keyboard. It says, "You will be a lion in your own cause". It came from a fortune cookie just about one year ago. I recall taping it to my laptop as inspiration to keep me motivated while searching for a new job and writing this book. Of course, my wife yapping at me to "finish the book!" was motivating too! I guess this "fortune" hit home because I am a Leo, thus the lion. I also believe in personal responsibility (thanks mom and dad), and, I love Chinese food.

So in the past few months I've practiced what I preach and have been a lion in my own cause. After evaluating a number of opportunities, I have landed; which I will discuss a bit later. More importantly, I've recognized there are things I've been meaning to do and found excuses to put them off. There is no time for excuses. My children are grown and on their own with spouses, homes and careers. I've been in corporate America for 33 years. I've climbed the corporate ladder and having achieved that goal, I've gained a much better understanding of myself, my abilities, and goals in life.

Do I owe a debt of gratitude to those who determined I was no longer necessary and my legacy will live on? Ok, let's not get crazy here, but I will say that had I not had this life changing event, I may not have changed my life.

I used to sing, I used to sing a lot, and I love to sing. I've been reminded recently how much I enjoy doing this. In spite of my love of singing, I stopped long ago as I began to raise a family, build a career, continue my education, advance my career, etc. Recently, I had the opportunity, while searching for a new job, to do some singing (performing with some old friends). I realized how much I missed this in my life so I am going to continue to make time to sing in addition to my "landing".

Well, exactly one year to the day of being fired, I accepted a position with a physician practice just minutes from my home. One of the physicians, a friend and a part of my network, contacted me one evening to see if I would be interested in speaking with the managing partners (physicians) about taking on the role of executive director with the practice. The ironies associated with this opportunity abound! More on that later.

Prior to receiving this call from my friend, I had a few "irons in the fire". One of these was in an area which I thought could be a perfect capstone to my career–business coaching. During my research, I contacted a number of companies in the executive coaching business. I selected one company to pursue with whom I was impressed and I just happened to know a number of their coaches, as well as executives being coached. I went through an extensive interviewing process and eventually was asked to become part of the organization. I was to attend their one week training program in California to become familiar with their system. Although this is an international firm, I could become an executive coach in my geographical region.

I was very interested in this opportunity; one I had not given any thought to prior to my "journey", and was seriously considering attending the training in March 2010. I felt then and feel now that the idea of coaching, whether at the executive or mid-management level, would be the perfect end to my business and leadership career. The idea of assisting others, in not only developing their leadership skills, but seeking a balanced quality of life, seemed like a terrific way to fulfill my desire to share my knowledge and give back to those who may benefit from my over three decades of experience.

My consideration of this alternative was *timing*. The economics associated with this company's program require the coach, with some assistance from the corporation, to solicit executives to become a part of the group and in fact develop a membership of 12-14 executives. This typically takes at least 6 months and there is a 50% failure rate to keeping a group together. So there is an economic risk. You are an independent contractor and therefore, you receive no benefits (e.g. health insurance, life insurance, pension, etc). This is not necessarily an issue if you have a spouse who works full-time and is covered by a health plan, or if you are receiving Medicare benefits. In my situation, it would be a greater risk than I was willing to take at this point in my life. I continue to believe that this will be a very attractive option in about 5 years or so.

This decision speaks to the subject I discussed earlier in the book. It is important to weigh your options, research all aspects of an opportunity, and then take action if you are comfortable with the risk and reward. It is not in your best interest to jump at the first thing that comes along. Granted, there may come a time when you may need to commit in order to survive, but keep in mind that you might create a chain of events and subsequent job changes which at the end of the day, works against you. As I was evaluating the coaching option other alternatives presented themselves (consulting, acquiring a business, and becoming a physician practice administrator.)

Back to the ironies I alluded to earlier. When I was terminated from my position, a position in healthcare, I thought, "I need to get out of healthcare." I was asked in the very early stages of my journey if I would consider managing a physician practice? To this question, I said, "Heck no!" I couldn't see myself working for multiple physician owners, dealing with numerous bosses, each with their own particular projects and approaches to the *business* of healthcare—"never happen". And, staying in my existing market I would have business dealings with my previous employer—"no way".

I guess you should *"never say never!"* I accepted the position as Executive Director of a 14 physician specialty practice. I work closely with the health system that fired me, in fact, my corporate office is located within the complex owned and operated by my previous employer—a facility for which I used to be responsible! This is either irony or someone has a bizarre sense of humor.

Why am I elaborating on all this? It's because I believe my "landing" speaks to many aspects touched on throughout this book—it can happen to you too! When you are first sent on your journey and you think, "this is the end of my career as I know it" and it feels like a devastating conclusion to your otherwise successful career, this is not the end! How do I say this? As I went through this journey, I:

- Reconnected with old friends
- Had the opportunity to consult
- Began writing a book (this book) & started planning my next
- Evaluated a number of career alternatives
- Learned a great deal about myself
- Reconnected with something I've always wanted to do
- "Landed" a new career with an extraordinary healthcare organization

The group with whom I work is not only a well-established specialty physician practice, but as executive director, the physicians allow me to run the business and make decisions on their behalf. This position incorporates my background in healthcare, small business experience, real estate management, knowledge of the community, and personal and business relationships along with an understanding of the major health systems in the region.

The position also allows me to develop the organization's culture and utilize my skills in coaching and staff development. This opportunity turned out to be a good fit all around and speaks to adaptability and being open to possibilities.

An interesting dynamic was created with respect to my current employer's offices being situated within the facility for which I was previously responsible. This presented the opportunity for me to reconnect with many of my former staff. Instead of "hiding" in my office, which would have been the easier thing to do (at least in the early days), I walked confidently though the facility, kept my head held high, and engaged everyone I had the opportunity to run into. Many were delighted to see my "return" and were pleased I had "landed". One former employee, a manager, said he admired my strength to return in this new role and put my pride and ego aside. It didn't sound so good when he said it, but having known him for years, I knew he meant well and what he was trying to say. I could have passed up a great opportunity if I allowed myself to let my ego stand in the way. If you are faced with a similar type of decision you need to put emotion aside in order to make the right decision for you and your family.

And the final irony—I need to work closely and build a positive relationship with the same individuals and organization that had determined my services were not longer needed.

It is said "time heals all wounds." I'm not certain of that but it can be said, the person who rises above the fray and *practices* ethics (not just *preach* them) will show the true content of his character.

One year has passed since accepting the executive director position at the specialty physician practice where the work has allowed me to capitalize on the breadth of my professional experience. It has proven to be a good decision. In addition, I plan to continue developing my coaching skills and expand my experience, sing as opportunities present themselves (my wife is my agent), and write my next book.

I am comfortable knowing where I've been, where I am today, and where I plan to go. If I can achieve this peace of mind and spirit, so can you. Is there an option out there which you refrained from considering at any other time in your former career? Can you imagine a change in lifestyle? Can you make this an opportunity to improve your quality of life? Can you survive financially and perhaps do something you always dreamed of doing? Can you lead a productive, *balanced* life with less income? Is it time to start winding down and dialing back the number of work hours?

Remember, "Landing on Your Feet" does not mean finding an exact position which mirrors the one you once had. It can be finding a way of life that meets your expectations for the future, perhaps a future you weren't quite ready to experience, but may be a blessing overall.

I welcome your comments and hearing about your journey and invite you to post your comments and experiences at, www.youwilllandonyourfeet.com. I wish you all the best as you journey through this process and hope this book helps you *"land softly"*.

> *"Think you can, think you can't; either way you'll be right."* ~**Henry Ford**

Appendix:
Business Acquisition
Due-Diligence Checklist

COMPANY
- How many years has the company been in business?
- What are the stated purposes for the sale?
- Is the company dependant on copyrights, patents, or customer lists?
- How important is the current owner to the success of the business?
- What is the nature of the business? (retailing product to consumers, real estate sales, manufacturing, mail order, etc.)
- What phase is the business in? (start up; expansion, cash generator, mature market)
- What is the existing structure? (LLC, corporation, partner-ship, etc.)

PRODUCTS AND SERVICES
- What is the current product or service line?
- What makes the products or services unique?
- How is the pricing of products or services relative to competitors?
- Is there a risk of obsolescence?
- Are new products or services needed to maintain competitive edge?
- What are the service capabilities versus competition?
- What is the profitability of each key product/service line?
- Does the product require trademark or servicemark protection?

MARKET RELATED
- What does the competition do differently?
- Who are the 5 largest competitors ranked by sales?
- How does the company differentiate its products or services from those of the competition?
- Has the number of competitors increased or decreased in the last 2 years, and is it expected to change in the future?
- What is company's market share?
- What is the company's reputation in the marketplace?
- Who are the key customers (over 5% of the revenue)?
- Is demand seasonal?
- What is the current and/or anticipated market share over the next 5 years (e.g., 25%, 30%)?
- What geographical area will be served?
- What is the marketing strategy?
- Is there currently a sales force?
- What are the distribution channels?
- Is R&D important to defend existing market and/or to create new ones?
- How are customer relations handled?

MANAGEMENT
- What is the organizational structure?
- What are the strengths of the management team?
- How would the overall style of management be characterized?
- Does the company employ any independent contractors?
- Are any employees members of labor unions?
- What benefits are offered to employees?

OPERATIONS
- What key vendors are supplying 10% (or greater) of total supplies?
- Is there any pending litigation against the company?
- How many times does the inventory turn?
- Is the facility owned or rented?

- Are any facilities obsolete?
- Is product or service liability a significant issue?
- What type of insurance coverage is required?
- What is the current production or services level capacity?
- Can the current or proposed facility handle future growth demands?
- How long before capital expenditures will be needed to meet excess demand?
- Does the company have all necessary licenses, building and operating permits?

FINANCIAL ANALYSIS

- What is the total current A/R?
- What is the average amount of Accounts Payable?
- What is the 3 year financial history of the income statements, balance sheets, and cash flow?
- What is the 3 year projected financials and assumptions underlying the projections?
- What is the current net operating income?
- What is the break-even point?
- What is the monthly cash burn rate, and how will it fluctuate pre and post funding?
- What is the greatest risk in investing in this company?
- What is the exit strategy if the business does not meet expectations?

NOTE: To purchase a comprehensive Merger, Acquisition and Joint Venture Analysis Checklist, go to www.rennaconsulting.net.

www.ingramcontent.com/pod-product-compliance
Lightning Source LLC
Chambersburg PA
CBHW020609300526
45785CB00021B/1285